Demetrios Vikelas, Joannes Gennadius

Loukis Laras

Reminiscences of a Chiote merchant during the war of independence

Demetrios Vikelas, Joannes Gennadius
Loukis Laras
Reminiscences of a Chiote merchant during the war of independence

ISBN/EAN: 9783337115609

Printed in Europe, USA, Canada, Australia, Japan

Cover: Foto ©ninafisch / pixelio.de

More available books at **www.hansebooks.com**

LOUKIS LARAS

*REMINISCENCES OF
A CHIOTE MERCHANT DURING THE
WAR OF INDEPENDENCE*

By D. BIKELAS

TRANSLATED FROM THE GREEK

By J. GENNADIUS

London
MACMILLAN & CO.
1881

Printed by R. & R. CLARK, *Edinburgh.*

PREFACE.

THE translation into English of a modern Greek tale is a literary enterprise so unusual, not to say unprecedented, that it seems to call for some explanation, if not for apology.

Loukis Laras appeared for the first time as a serial in that excellent Athenian periodical, the *Hestia*, during the early part of 1879. The popularity to which it rapidly attained rendered necessary its publication in a separate volume, and a second edition is already announced, a compliment not often paid to a book issued within the restricted limits of Greece.

The merits of the work, however, were not long in being recognised by a wider circle of readers—those Greek scholars in the west of Europe who have given their special attention to the Mediæval and Neohellenic epochs of Greek literature.

The distinguished Hellenist, the Marquis de Queux de Saint-Hilaire, published last year, in Paris, a French translation, which elicited, in favour of M. Bikelas's work, so high an opinion from those who had occasion to comment on it, that Loukis Laras has been included in the official list of books to be placed in the popular libraries, and to be awarded as prizes in the French Lycées.

A German translation soon followed; it is the work of William Wagner, whose premature death has since left in the ranks of Hellenic scholars a gap not readily to be filled up.

In Italy and in Denmark translations have also appeared—in the latter country from the pen of Professor Jean Pio; and the author has had more than one application for translations in other languages.

So rapid and so unusual a success of a work written in an idiom which, to say the least, finds no place in the curriculum of general studies, would, in itself, have been a sufficient warranty for this translation. But, moreover, both the original of Loukis Laras passed the best part of his life and ended his days in England, and our author himself became known in London as a man of business at first, and later on as a man of letters also.

M. Bikelas, while sacrificing to Hermes, the promoter of commerce, was faithful to the god under his no less glorious attribute of protector of learning. Following up, in this respect, a family tradition, and being prompted by hereditary talent, he soon made a beginning in poetry, and a collection of his earlier verses was printed in 1862 in London. Ten years later another instalment of occasional pieces was issued at Athens, including translations into modern Greek of the Sixth

Book of the Odyssey, the Garden Scene of Goethe's *Faust,* and a humorous tirade, entitled "The Greeks of Old." This latter poem was translated into German by A. Ellissen (*Magazine für die Litteratur des Auslandes,* vol. lxv.)

But this innate tendency towards poetic pursuits in no way impeded the development of more solid scholarly qualities.

In issuing a Greek translation of M. Egger's essay *On the Language and Nationality of the Modern Greeks* (London, 1864), M. Bikelas set forth his opinions as to the vexed and still unsolved question of style and degree of purity to be aimed at in the written language of to-day. And in 1871 he published a lecture on Mediæval and Recent Greek Literature which he had delivered at the Hellenic College in London.

To the pursuit of such researches he now applied himself with increasing perseverance; and two years later, while still in the prime of life, he was enabled—happily for Greek literature no less than for himself—to realise his desire and ultimate aim in this direction. Abandoning commerce, from which he had derived such benefits of independence and comfort as can alone render that vocation attractive to men of higher culture, he returned to Greece, and has since devoted himself exclusively to literature.

In 1874 he published a short but very remarkable essay on the political status of the Greeks of Byzantium and their influence on mediæval culture in Europe. This work, the substance of which was first delivered in three lectures to the Greek Syllogos at Marseilles, attracted considerable attention both in France and Germany. In the former country it was at once translated by M. Emile Legrand (*Les Grecs au Moyen Age, Étude historique;* Paris, Maisonneuve), and in 1878 a German translation appeared from the pen of Professor Wagner, which met with high praise from Professor F. Hirsch in the *Mittheilungen aus der historischen Litteratur.*

But the most important, thus far, and for Englishmen perhaps the most interesting, production of our author, are his metrical translations of several of Shakespeare's plays. In this he has displayed consummate skill in versification, great resource and mastery of language, a most intimate acquaintance with the intricacies of the great dramatist, and a thorough appreciation of the beauties and subtleties of his idiom, which to a Greek translator often presents difficulties almost insuperable. "Romeo and Juliet," "Othello," and "King Lear" were published at Athens (London, Williams and Norgate), and a second volume, containing "Hamlet" and "Macbeth," is announced.

The continued success which the previous attempts of our author met with has been surpassed by the work before us, possessing as it does the additional merit of complete originality.

The short intimation prefatory to the first chapter may, in fact, be considered only as a novelist's device. It is true in substance; but the MS. notes left by the prototype of *Loukis Laras* were of the most elementary and meagre description, and our author has created both the simple but interesting plot which exists in the work, and most of the persons of the story.

Nevertheless he has succeeded in disappearing so completely behind the impersonation of his hero, who is delineated in so artless and yet so vivid a manner, that the timid, awkward, and not over-winning, yet sympathetic and talkative Loukis, misleads the reader into the belief that he is actually listening to the simple narrative of the old merchant.

The grace and the free flow of the style render it—even for those who may differ on particular points—a model of what may be considered the unaffected and normal condition of the Greek of to-day. And therefore the Syllogos for the Propagation of Greek Literature have adopted Loukis Laras as a reading-book in their schools.

Yet the delineation of character is lifelike, the descriptions vivid, and the whole economy of the work skilful. We cannot speak of its plot, for it has hardly any. But the story, which is substantially a true one, is dramatic and stirring. Loukis Laras lives in the most eventful period of modern Greek history — the War of Liberation; and, although, both by temperament and circumstances, he is precluded from taking an active part in the life-and-death struggle in which the Greek nation was then engaged, he is a sufferer from its consequences, and a faithful narrator of the heroic deeds and the martyrdom of his countrymen. His is certainly not the noblest of characters, but perhaps on that account he serves the better to demonstrate the heroism of those around him.

Those who are unacquainted with the works, not of Greek historians alone, but of Blaquiere, Finlay, Gordon, Gervinus, and Hertzberg, can hardly realise the superhuman efforts and sacrifices with which the Greeks achieved even the little they now possess; they can hardly conceive what rivers of blood and what myriads of victims Turkish ferocity —then still unimpaired by exhaustion, and unrestrained by European interference—extorted as the price of that small concession.

It is necessary to address this reminder to those readers of the following pages who may feel inclined to tax our author with exaggeration. He has erred, indeed, but, as it was natural to expect from him, he has erred on the side of moderation.

His work is, on the whole, scrupulously true to historic facts. Yet it can hardly be called an historical romance. It is rather a graphic narrative of individual experiences during times of great national convulsions, very much akin to the *Romans Nationaux* of Erckmann-Chatrian.

It may not be amiss to offer, at this stage of our remarks, a very succinct account of Neohellenic romance-writing. We cannot refer the reader to any safe guide on this point. The latest attempt at a history of modern Greek literature—that of M. Rangabis, now Greek Envoy at Berlin, and one of the most brilliant poets and authors the last generation has produced—can hardly be considered a reliable and scientific treatise. The author himself acknowledges in his preface that he composed it hastily and from undigested notes. Another work in German, by Herr Nicolay, is not more than a rather incoherent catalogue. The *Cours de Litterature Grecque Moderne* (Genève, 1828), by Rizo Néroulos, though excellent as far as it goes, is out of date. And M. Gidel's two masterly series of *Études sur la Litterature Grecque Moderne* (Paris, 1866 and 1878), the former of which was "Couronée en 1864, par l'Academie des Inscriptiones et Belles Lettres," refer rather to mediæval Greek literature. An acceptable account of what has since been accomplished still remains a desideratum; and in compiling these few notes, we thought we could do no better than follow the lines so ably traced out by the late Professor William Wagner.

It was but natural that the events of the Revolution should have served as the theme of almost every successful modern Greek novel. That epoch is the one which offers an inexhaustible store of thrilling episodes; which has left the most vivid and lasting impressions on the mind of the people, and which has fused and reformed national life and character.

Still, it is not possible to cite much in this branch of Neohellenic literature; nor was it to be expected that novel-writing, which is in all countries the luxuriant and superabundant efflorescence of letters, and which presupposes a large and wealthy circle of readers, should have preceded in Greece the appearance of other forms of literature of a more substantial character and a more pressing need. The love of the beautiful, for beauty's sake alone, and for the pleasure it procures, can only be developed by slow degrees and by the prevalence of ease.

Poetic narrative, however, sprang up at a very early stage of modern Greek literature: some of the earliest national songs still in the mouths of the people, dating as far back as immediately after the fall of Constantinople (A.D. 1453). And since then, the whole life and vigour of the nation has been reflected and nurtured by those grand and truly epic songs, which form the text of the works of Fauriel, Marcellus, Tomaseo, and Passow.

But artistic prose and fiction writing has hardly yet been fully developed in Modern Greece. Those who may be said to have really introduced it amongst us are the brothers Alexander and Panagiotis Soutzos, who flourished during the disturbed times immediately following the Revolution.

The direction of the affairs of the State, and the guidance of public opinion, such as then existed, necessarily fell to the almost exclusive keeping, not of trained statesmen, but of these few men who had attained to some literary eminence; and the two brothers Soutzos, being endowed with remarkable poetic talents, could not help being politicians rather than poets. There exists, therefore, little of their prose or verse which does not aim directly at some political object.

Alexander Soutzos especially was a man of rare genius as a poet, and his verses, notwithstanding their irredeemably factious tendency, remain to this day the most fresh and stirring of Neohellenic metrical writings. He was a master of language, and his satirical acumen was the most dreaded political weapon of those days.

It was in such a spirit and with similar objects that he conceived "The Exile of 1831" (published 1835), which is more of a political essay than a pure work of fiction. The author apparently was not concerned with the characters which he presented to the reader, but used them simply to convey his own political theories. The hero is well delineated; but Aspasia, the heroine, is a weak creature, and does not occupy much of the reader's attention.

Similar in tendency is the "Leandros" (1834) of the elder brother Panagiotis, who, however, adopted the monotonous and tedious form of epistolary narrative, in close imitation of Werther and the Letters of Jacobo Ortis. Leandros is discontented with himself and the circumstances of his country; nor is he more fortunate in love. For Coralia, to whom he was attached in youth, he now finds the mother of a large family; and they both die without meeting in this life with the happiness they sought for. Ch. A. Brandiss, in his *Mittheilungen aus Griechenland* (1842), gives a full analysis of this work, which lacks action but is full of fine passages and descriptions often beautiful.

Such are the prose writings of the two Soutzos, who, although they produced interesting theoretical essays rather than real works of fiction, yet have marked out the line to be followed by those of their successors who would create something of an original and genuine character. They confined themselves to the life of the nation; they were imbued with its traditions, and they took their characters from the people amongst whom they lived. They failed in elaboration. But there was nothing hybrid, incongruous, or affected in their writings.

The author who has since followed closest upon their traces is M. Rangabis, whose prolific pen has given us a considerable number of more or less short narratives. In the *Prince of the Morea*, the most important of them both in substance and length, and which has been translated into German by Ellissen, he has laid his rather intricate plot in a most interesting epoch of Greek mediæval history, but the description he gives of the condition of the Greeks of the Morea during the thirteenth century is more vivid and poetic than historically accurate.

He has treated of more modern times in his *Notary* and the *Excursion to Poros;* and in both these tales his pictures of Greek life of about thirty or forty years ago are accurate and pleasing. In his other tales he has borrowed subjects from foreign prototypes.

M. Rangabis' style is flowing, though much given to the reproduction of Gallicisms in Greek words. But he is a good observer of his people, and his vivacity and intimate knowledge of all the artifices of authorship, often make us forget the inherent shallowness of his work.

M. G. Palæologos' only novel, the *Painter*, is lifelike in its descriptions, able in the delineation of character, and pure in style.

The tales of M. Ramphos, and especially his *Halet Effendi*, transport us to a purely Eastern world. They are often humorous, and always skilful and true to nature in the scenes they describe.

M. Ambellas' patriotic novel *Helena of Miletos*, and M. Salabanda's historical novel on Souli, may also be mentioned.

Another Greek gentleman, long resident in England, M. Stephanos Xenos, has proved himself no less prolific with the pen than active in commerce. *The Devil in Turkey* (1851) he translated himself into English; and his *Heroine of the Greek Revolution* (London, 1861) is a work of considerable merit. Though at times confused and not very methodical, his writings display talent and great vivacity, abound in exciting scenes, and contain some excellent passages.

Very different from all its predecessors is M. Roïdis' work, *The Popess Joanna*. The subject is undoubtedly one which presents great difficulties of treatment, and the author has not always been able to avoid what may be considered as dangerous ground. But the work itself displays considerable ability; while the historical preface is an evidence of deep study of the times to which it refers. The style is fluent and agreeable; and a French translation followed soon after the publication of the Greek text, which has also been translated into German by Herr W. Fest (Leipzig, 1873).

Although less pretentious than any of the tales and novels we have quoted, *Loukis Laras* is more remarkable than its predecessors on many grounds, as we believe the foregoing remarks will have shown. It marks a fresh and more healthy departure in modern Greek Literature. The matter compressed within its two hundred pages contains substance sufficient to make up the regulation three-volume novel. Much creative power has been displayed in the moulding of the very meagre facts which have served as the basis of the work. Its sentiment is tender, without lack of a strong imagination. And the underlying sense of quiet humour is no less pleasing than the absence of any political cavil. Finally, as a specimen of the actual Greek prose style, it is more even and perfect than anything produced of late years.

We do not pretend to have succeeded in rendering sufficient justice to the elegance of the Greek original by a translation undertaken amidst many other pressing occupations. Greek and English cannot easily be rendered, the one language into the other; and some of our shortcomings may be the result of a desire to reproduce the shades of the original so accurately as to render it available, with the help of this translation, as a text-book for those who wish to give some attention to the modern form of the Greek language.

Some notes have been added, explanatory of allusions in the text, which would otherwise have remained unintelligible to the English reader. We have followed in this respect the example of the German and French translations, to the latter of which the author himself supplied these elucidations. But many fresh notes have now been added.

J. G.

PALL MALL,
December 1880.

LOUKIS LARAS.

THOSE of our countrymen who have resided in England will easily recognise the old Chiote merchant, who is here concealed under the name of Loukis Laras. Often have I heard him relate the vicissitudes of his early years; and it was at my suggestion that, towards the close of his life, he undertook to write his memoirs. When, a few years ago, he died, his manuscript notes were found amongst his papers under cover, addressed to me. In publishing them now, I wish they may be read by others with as great an interest and pleasure as I experienced whenever I listened to the narration of the old gentleman.

I.

IN the early part of the year 1821 I resided at Smyrna. I was then nearly twenty years of age; and seven years had already elapsed since my master, Pappa Floutis—may God have mercy on his soul!—assured my father that I then knew quite as much as was necessary for a man destined to a business career. My father, either convinced by what the good old monk told him, or, perhaps, because he considered the training of a practical life more useful to me, did not think fit that I should continue my studies at Chio, but took me to his house of business at Smyrna, first as an apprenticed clerk, and shortly afterwards as a partner.

Time went on, and the Almighty blessed our labours. Our balance grew larger on each successive year, and our credit became more and more firmly established in the market of Smyrna. Besides, and I may say this with no unreasonable pride, my father had from the outset acquired for himself an honourable reputation, and enjoyed great consideration; he was a man of the strictest probity, and most scrupulous in his dealings. I may add—not in self praise, but as a tribute of filial gratitude—that my success in life and in commerce I owe, above all, to those principles of honesty which my father inculcated upon me from very childhood.

As our profits increased so the circle of our operations became more extended, and, at the same time, our plans for the future were developed. Relations at second hand with correspondents in Europe no longer satisfied our commercial activity. Two or three of our fellow-islanders—the Columbuses of Greek commerce—had about that time pitched their tent in London. Their successes allowed us no rest, and their example fanned the flame of our ambition.

It was therefore decided that in the autumn I should proceed to England, accompanied by a maternal uncle of mine. Indeed, I had begun learning English from a clergyman—a kind of Pappa Floutis—who, however, did not succeed in imparting to me much of that language. But perhaps the fault did not rest entirely with him. Let me not inveigh against the memory of my earliest teachers.

My father and I, as in fact all our relations and friends at Smyrna, were devoted heart and soul to our business. Of the Hetæria, or of a projected insurrection, we knew nothing. It is true that we, in common with all the Greeks of that time, experienced a vague longing after liberty. We saw around us at Smyrna the subjects of European States hold their heads erect, and it was with a feeling of latent bitterness that we almost envied the freedom which the other nations of Christendom enjoyed. We had some dim notions of the events of the French Revolution, and we even cherished an undefined hope of national restoration, based principally on the expectation of help from the North; and on great festivals we also sung at our family gatherings the songs of Rhigas. But we never dreamt for a moment that we were on the eve of a national uprising.

We passed our uneventful existence in the khan, busy by day with our motley stock of goods, and at night shut up in our small room, over the warehouse, where my father and I slept. On Sundays we went regularly to the liturgy in the Church of Saint Photini, and sometimes, on our way back, we called on the Chiote families then resident at Smyrna. Rarely—perhaps once or twice in the year, during the Easter holidays—we ventured on some excursion as far as the surrounding villages: and there, in the freshness of the country air, in the fields and under shady trees, we thought of Chio, and of our tower and our own garden; and the separation from our home then seemed to us more hard to bear.

Thus one day succeeded another, and time rolled on. But my main thought was still the projected voyage to England: it had become my constant dream; and a golden dream it was, in every sense of the word. Suddenly, however, both tranquillity and business, both projects and dreams, were all at once overturned.

One night, in the beginning of March, I awoke startled with fear. I had heard in my sleep repeated firing of guns. I sat up in my bed, with ears intent on catching every sound, and with eyes staring in the darkness. My father was fast asleep. Was I dreaming? No! . . . The firing recommenced, and at the same time wild cries filled the air. I awoke my father, and we both listened. All through the night the firing and the tumult continued at intervals; but we could not imagine what had occurred. And how were we to know? Curiosity prompted us to venture out, but fear got the better of us and kept us shut up in our room.

At dawn we went down stairs into the

square of the khan, and there we found gathered others of our neighbours, all in the same state of bewilderment and anxiety.

The khans are generally built like small fortresses. On the outside rise high and solid walls, enclosing an open courtyard, square or oblong, as the case may be, and on this central court open the doors and windows of the warehouses and apartments built around. Communication with the outside world is kept up through an iron gate, which is closed at night.

When, in the morning, the watchman opened this gate, we were informed that the previous evening orders had arrived bidding the Turks arm themselves. Hence their war-cries and the firing during the night. But arm, for what purpose? What danger prompted this order? We inquired of those who came to us in the Khan, but we could get no precise answer. One said the Janissaries had revolted; another that war with Russia had broken out; some whispered that the Christians had risen.

So passed that day. It was a Saturday. We had not gone outside the khan, but from the gate we could see the Turks walking up and down the streets, armed to the teeth, and looking very fierce.

Next morning we went as usual to Church. On that Sunday there was to be no sermon, so that the congregation were surprised to see the priest mount the pulpit. It was not, however, in order to preach the word of God, but in order to read a Patriarchal excommunication. We all listened in stupefaction to the recital of those terrible maledictions and fearful anathemas. We heard the names of Ypsilanti and Soutzos mentioned, as of men guilty of treason; and we gathered that all this related to insurrectionary movements in Walachia, or to some secret conspiracy.

We looked at each other amazed: whispers, inquiries, and cross-questions soon filled the church. What was the meaning of this insurrection which was thus anathematised? What was its origin? We only knew for certain that Ypsilanti held a high position in Russia, and we somehow inferred that the movement originated in that quarter, and that it was the prelude to a Russo-Turkish war. But all these conjectures passed through our minds in a very vague and confused form—much more so than I can now describe.

The Turks at Smyrna were themselves still in the dark as to what had occurred, nor had they quite realised the fact that the rayahs had risen spontaneously and unaided. They thought that the danger came from the side of Russia. None the less, their fanaticism was aroused instantly on the first reports. War against the infidels was imminent: consequently every Christian was an enemy, and every rayah a victim ready to land. Things therefore looked very black for us from the very first day, and our minds were weighed down with anxiety and fear.

These words: anxiety, fear, have already more than once escaped my pen. But why should I try to display a courage which we neither felt nor could have possessed? Do not smile, my good reader, recollecting I am a Chiote, and do not attribute my timidity to a temperament commonly imputed to my compatriots. I should like to have seen you then in my place, however brave you may fancy yourself! Unarmed, defenceless, unprotected, cowed down with servitude, exposed to the violence or the sword of the first Turk whose temper might have been ruffled, with no hope of justice or even of revenge—how could we, the insignificant traders of the khan at Smyrna, how could we be imbued with any feelings of courage? In what stead would courage have stood us? We had only patience, and much we needed it, for our life from this time became a protracted agony, a continuous martyrdom. But even patience has its limits; and when it is exhausted, there sets in either complete prostration, or that kind of despair which leads on to heroism. Many heroic incidents, both during the Greek revolution, and at other times in the history of man, were perhaps but the result of such despair! God preserved me from complete prostration, and nature had not fitted me for acts of heroic despair. But then, I never quite lost either patience or hope; and for this I often thank the Most High.

A few days after that Sunday of the excommunication, I went one morning to the quarter of the Jews in order to collect moneys due to us. I had received payment of a certain sum, and was making secure in my pocket the bag containing the money, when suddenly I heard shouts and the sound of rapid steps, and I saw a stream of Christians and Jews flying towards us. Before our Hebrew customer had time to shut the door, his dark warehouse was filled with terror-stricken Jews. The incoherent words they whispered in their Spanish patois did not explain matters, and hardly reassured me. They themselves did not quite know what had happened, and why they had been put to flight.

The tumult, however, having subsided, and the outside world appearing again quiet, we stealthily opened the door. The other shops were gradually being opened, and those who had there found shelter began to take heart and make their appearance; so that at length, communicated from mouth to mouth, the true cause of the scare was made known. A camel, laden with bales of cotton, missed its footing, and falling in the narrow street of the bazaar, broke the door of a shop. The noise of the shattered door, the shouts of the drivers, and of the Jews inside the shop, the crowd which gathered around the prostrate camel—this turmoil was at once misinterpreted as the beginning of a riot, and the attendant confusion resulted in a panic and a general stampede.

When the necessary predisposition exists in men's minds, it does not take much to create a panic: and, unfortunately, there were but strong reasons for such a predisposition. The excitement of the Turks increased daily. It was known that they held nightly meetings in their quarter, and threats had been heard of an impending attack on the Christians. But as yet I was not informed of all this, so that I was not prepared for fresh emotions on that day.

I therefore took leave of my Hebrew friends. I folded my dress over my chest, for better security of the bag I had placed in my pocket, and I sallied forth on my way home. I had hardly turned into the main street when I again heard shouts and yells, and before I had time to stand aside and find shelter, I was surrounded by Turks, who, sword in hand, swarmed on every side, and rushed on furiously. How I escaped being trampled under foot, how they did not kill me, I cannot comprehend to this day. The current swept me along, and I ran with them. I gathered kicks on one side, fist-cuffs on the other; but I ran on senseless with fear, knowing neither where I went nor what would become of me. I did not even consider this. The whole thing was like a fearful dream. I knew well the streets of Smyrna, but I could not then distinguish which streets we traversed, nor can I now remember. I only recollect that at a turn of the road I saw, opposite, the door of our Khan, and I recognised it. It was half shut; I don't know how I got inside it,—in my room,—near my father.

All this remains confused in my memory. But when I opened my eyes I found myself stretched on my bed, and panting; my father stood bent over me and bathed my head with cold water. I remember feeling a great weight on my chest, and then only I thought of the bag; and laying my hand in my bosom I lifted it off me.

I cannot forget my father's smile when I handed to him the bag. I then interpreted it as a mark of satisfaction at the safety of the money. But when I, in my turn, became a father, then I understood its true significance. "What is money to me, now? It is of thee, my son, I am concerned!"

Such was the meaning of that smile. For my father loved me; he loved me dearly. He never told me so; nor did he show his affection by demonstrations of effusive tenderness. It was only when he died, and he was no longer near me, that on recollecting our vicissitudes and the various incidents of the life we passed together during many years, it was only then I comprehended and fully appreciated the degree of his affection for me.

Why is this so? Is it because we must lose something in order to know all it is worth? Or because later misfortunes and sufferings had enlightened my mind and had made my heart grow larger?

But those Turks, what were they bent upon? As I learnt afterwards, they were going to the Frankish quarter of the town with foul designs upon those who lived there. Fortunately the Pacha succeeded in pacifying them, and there was nothing to lament that day. The actual reign of terror had not yet set in.

Nevertheless, that tumult, the first demonstration of armed Turks against Christians, my first conception of real danger, remained impressed on my memory more vividly, perhaps, than anything I saw or suffered subsequently.

From that day the Turks became more aggressive. Blood had not yet been shed, but the insults, the threats, the angry looks, the ostentatious display of arms, were all terrible premonitions of the coming storm.

The state of things became more grave as the insurrection spread. Each shout for freedom on the part of the Greeks was answered by a fresh outburst of Turkish fanaticism, until at length there was an end to all constraint; and the Turks, maddened with frenzy, butchered and pillaged and made slaves by the thousand.

News did not reach us either regularly or accurately; but somehow the echo of those first throbs of national resurrection penetrated into the seclusion of our khan. Thus we learnt what had occurred in Walachia; thus we heard, one day, that the Morea had risen in insurrection, that the Archbishop of Patræ and the primates of the Peloponnesus had placed themselves at the head of the movement; and at the same time the rumour went round that Hydra and Spetzæ had revolted.

When my mind reverts to that glorious past, when I think over the incidents and inquire into my own impressions at that time, and I examine them as a reflex, so to say, of the public feeling of those days, I often come to this conclusion, that the participation of our naval islands in the national struggle at its very commencement contributed to strengthen and propagate the insurrection perhaps more than most men can now conceive.

And this I say, not so much with reference to the very important material support which the Greek navy afforded to the nation; nor with reference to the magnificent achievements which won for the Greek name a fresh crown of immortal glory. No. These things we witnessed and understood later on. But from the very first we, who lived at a distance from the centre of national upheaval, when we heard that the mariners of Hydra, Spetzæ, and Psara, had unfurled the flag of liberty, we realised more vividly what was the object in view. The captains of those islands represented, in a visible, so to say, and tangible manner, the national and panhellenic character of the revolution. For many of them were known to us, many were considered as friends; their names and their faces were familiar in every harbour, in every bazaar, in which Greeks were established. So that when we heard that these men, our acquaintances, our friends, were fighting for faith and fatherland, and had sworn either to win their freedom or die, we were all electrified more potently than when we first learnt of the attempt of Ypsilantis, or even of the rising in the Morea.

I refer to the early commencement of the struggle, and to our first impressions. Later on other causes made us feel how indissoluble were the ties which bound us to the insurgents. The Turks, by their indiscriminate massacres, their devastations, and the enslavement of peaceable men, of women and children, took care to remind us of the solidarity of our race, even if we were disposed to forget it.

Excuse, reader, these digressions. My pen, obedient to the impulses of an old man's heart, finds pleasure in loitering over the accumulated recollections of my sufferings and earlier impressions. My intention is to limit myself to the narrative of my own adventures in life. Yet the life of each one of us constitutes but a small unit, closely bound up with the total of the circumstances which encircle us. How am I to separate, in each instance, the vicissitudes of my insignificant self from the rush of the all-pervading whirlwind which carried me along! For this reason, and because I am an old man, perhaps I shall not always succeed in avoiding such digressions while writing my reminiscences. But neither are you, good reader, under an obligation to peruse them to the end.

When you were a child, and your nurse related to you her tales, she did so in order to gratify not only your curiosity, but also her own impulse which prompted her to repeat them. Sleep may have come over you sometimes. Yet she continued her tale, and you awoke just in time to listen to the finish. That is why you perhaps remember the beginning only and the end of many a fairy tale, though you may not know how the recollection of the middle portion has failed you. But my story has no particular beginning or end of its own; so that you may fall asleep even now: you will not interrupt me.

The first rumours of the insurrection reached us about Lent. What a Lent that was, and what an Easter that followed it! We went regularly to church, the more so as it was there that news circulated. They were often false, usually exaggerated; but still the only news we obtained. And let no one imagine that our concern with those events distracted our attention from the services of the Church. Far from it; the religious feeling was then strong. The sorrows of our nation became for us incarnate, so to say, in Christ's sufferings, and the impressive ritual of the Passion Week reflected faithfully the spiritual condition of the congregation.

About the middle of that week sinister rumours were heard. It was said that arrests and confiscations and massacres had taken place in Constantinople, and that many of the notables of the nation were beheaded. On Easter Sunday we learnt that the great Dragoman Mourousis was also put to death, and the dread of these successive reports cast a mournful veil over the cheering Collects of the Resurrection.

A few days later an appalling piece of news was spread about. The Patriarch had been hung! His body had been given over to the Jews to be insulted and outraged!

Our hearts now sank low and our knees shook under us. For we were overpowered by a twofold feeling—the horror which the sacrilege committed on the sacred person of the Patriarch, the chief of our nation, awakened in every Christian, in every Greek; and the conviction which gained strength, that the life of no one of us was any longer safe. If the very Government of the Sultan ventured upon such acts in the capital, and against the chiefs and notables of the people, what danger might not we, the worthless rayahs, apprehend from the unbridled ferocity of the Turks of Smyrna, and especially of those of Anatolia?

For days past swarms of savage irregulars had already begun to collect in the vicinity of Smyrna. Thirst for blood and booty had brought them together from the depths of Asia Minor. The Pacha appeared to have still some concern for the safety of the inhabitants, and kept his wild beasts outside the town. But their proximity aroused and excited the Smyrniot Turks, who thus became daily more menacing. From threats they were rapidly passing on to acts of violence; their hand was often laid on the dagger, and the dagger leapt from its sheath with increasing facility, so that many innocent men were wounded, and some murdered, in the streets of Smyrna.

Yet all this was but a prelude to the great sacrifice. The raving orgies supervened later on, when massacre, havoc, and slavery were rampant, not only in the streets and the bazaars, and in the houses of Christians, but under the very flags of the foreign consulates; nay, even on board European ships, whence hundreds of fugitives were carried away and put to death. But of these things I was informed subsequently. I did not witness them myself, and I do not wish to write but of what I saw and experienced.

In the meanwhile, many had begun to leave the country, even from the first days. Almost daily we heard that some one of our acquaintances had disappeared. What had become of him? Had he been put to death, or was he hiding for fear? At length it was ascertained that he had fled.

Now, the example of these fugitives, and the dread of dangers, steadily on the increase, left no peace to my father and myself. An irrepressible desire to leave the place took possession of us, and we thought of nothing but how to escape. This, however, became daily more difficult; the Turkish authorities no longer allowed the rayahs to leave. It was even said—but we would not yet credit it—that the consuls had received orders to turn back those who sought refuge on foreign ships. We did not believe it; yet it was true. Fortunately there were consuls and captains still left who had some sense of pity, and who would not become purveyors of victims to the Turks.

Things were in this state when Captain Bisbilis arrived at Smyrna. He was an old friend of my father's, and was in command of a schooner flying the Russian flag. No wonder my father breathed freely when he saw him enter the Khan. The good captain had come to offer us shelter in his ship, promising to take us to Chio in three days —immediately after discharging his cargo.

"To Chio!" I cried, on my father confiding to me his intention; "but shall we be safer there?"

"There at least we shall be with your mother and sisters. We shall either be spared with them, or else let us all perish together."

We began getting ready for departure. But we had neither time for preparations, nor did we wish to betray our project by ill-timed bustle. Therefore we decided to abandon our goods to the mercy of God, and our uncollected credits to the good faith of our debtors—provided they themselves survived those troubles. We only gathered all the ready money we could, and on the third day with beating hearts we awaited the sunset, as we had arranged with our friend the captain.

II.

The light of the sun had vanished, but darkness had not yet set in, when we shut our warehouse and left the khan. The gate was still open.

We carried with us neither bag nor parcel of any sort that could excite suspicion. We had only hidden in our pockets and under the folds of our garments the few things we might carry safely and unobserved. No one of our neighbours knew of our secret; yet, at that moment, it seemed to me as if the whole world was in possession of it. It seemed to me as if the doors, still half open, and the windows looking on the courtyard, had eyes which could penetrate through our clothes into the depths of our pockets, and deeper still, into the very thoughts of our hearts.

The old porter stood by the gate, his hands crossed behind him.

"How so late out of doors!" said he: "and where may you be going?"

"We are going to church," said my father.

Now it was neither the day nor the hour of vespers. I did not dare say a word to my father; but I felt convinced the old Turk had guessed we were decamping, and that he would go straightway and inform against us. Every shadow at a distance appeared to me as that of a Janissary or a Zeïbeg, sword in hand;—at every step I expected a sudden catastrophe.

Thank God, no untoward meeting interfered with our march. The captain had fixed where we should find him—at a remote corner of the town, and there he waited for us by the sea; the boat was a little farther on. The shore was desolate and perfectly still; the night quite dark. We jumped into the boat, and we were off.

It was only when we had got on board the ship that I felt my heart lighter and I breathed freely. Foreign ships had not as yet been seized by the Turks; so that, under the Russian flag of the schooner, I considered all immediate danger at an end. I fancied that once away from Smyrna we escaped all sufferings, dangers, and fears; and I did not then think of my first impression, namely, that by going to Chio we were by no means rid of the Turks. On the contrary, the more I considered the matter the more convinced I felt that there we would be quiet and safe. The few Turks in the island had gradually tamed down; in any case they were not numerous. The Chiotes were an industrious and peace-abiding people; and being prosperous and self-administered, they were the happiest of the Greeks at that time. Consequently, there was no probability, either of the insurrection spreading to Chio, or of the fury and fanaticism of the Turks exploding on its inhabitants.

I therefore contemplated calmly the preparations for our departure. The ship's anchor already hung by the bowsprit, and, as soon as we got on board, the boat was hoisted, the sails unfurled, and we were soon under weigh.

That night I slept soundly. Ever since, in the beginning of March, I had been startled by that wild firing, my sleep had become disturbed and interrupted; and latterly, the increase of insecurity and our plans of escape kept me awake, and many a night had passed in sleepless anxiety. But on board the good ship I felt safe. I thought at intervals of our frustrated journey to England; I recollected that fearful panic in the bazaar, when I ran on involuntarily, surrounded by Turks; I even fancied, now and then, I saw before me the patriarch hanging by the halter. But these unpleasant visions were soon dissipated by the sense of security, by the prospect of meeting my mother and sisters, and by the sweet reminiscences of my childhood.

Youth is naturally heedless and hopeful, and shrinks from dwelling on painful topics. The recollections of Smyrna soon vanished before the glow of comforting prospects, and I slumbered calmly, being rocked into sleep by the cadenced roll of the ship on the light waves, and by the creaking of her timbers.

When next morning I went on deck, the sun had hardly risen. Ahead of us we could just make out the island of Chio enveloped in a transparent morning mist. Far to our left, my father, stretching silently his hand, pointed out to me a long line of sails resting on the horizon like a covey of white doves. Old Captain Bisbilis—I fancy I see him before me as I write now—stood at the stern, his two hands curved over his brow, surveying attentively the distance, as if trying to count the ships.

"Are they coming or going?" asked my father.

"They are going towards Samos," said the captain. "May God be with them!"

"Amen!" answered my father, and the two old men made the sign of the cross.

Then for the first time the idea of the

revolution, the sense of national resurrection, was revealed to me as a living thing. Those white doves were the ships of the Greek fleet. The flag of the cross waved from their masts. They swept free over the Greek seas, manned by dauntless brave mariners, showing their flag from coast to coast, bidding the Christians take heart, and hurling defiance at the Turk. On that flag were inserted the words, "Freedom or death!"

When I saw the two old men so deeply impressed, I felt within me an indescribable emotion, the more hard to express as it was confused and uncertain. I felt as if my chest grew larger and my body taller. But it was a momentary and fleeting sensation; and, perhaps, writing now, I may be describing rather what I might have felt, than what I actually and precisely experienced.

A few hours later we landed at Chio.

I expected to find, as usual, the beach alive with people, to see friends and acquaintances at the landing-stage, to hear the cheering "welcome" and the good-natured banter which formerly on such occasions used to go on between those on shore and us in the boats. But the coffee-house by the jetty was empty, the quays deserted, the market-place desolate. Only here and there, standing by the doors of their shops, some silent and dejected tradesmen appeared to look at us with amazement, and saluted us as we passed on. The sight of that all-pervading gloom troubled me, and I felt inclined to ask those dispirited looking shopmen, "In the name of God, what has come to Chio? What has happened?" But I walked behind my father, following on his steps; it was not my habit to take the initiative when he was present.

Fortunately he himself could not be restrained much longer, and entering into the shop of an old acquaintance, he addressed to him, without any prefatory explanation as to our appearance, the very question which had come to my lips.

"A pretty time you have chosen to return, my friends; why, we have the end of the world upon us here."

Such were the first words of our old friend. But this melancholy reception did not interfere with his expressions of sincere pleasure at meeting my father again. He prevailed upon us to sit down; he insisted upon treating us to some refreshments, and, while thus receiving us hospitably, he related to us what had happened.

We then learned that the fleet which we had seen that morning, making for Samos, had remained ten days off the coast of Chio, under Admiral Tombazis, with the intention of provoking a rising in the island. But the Turks, as soon as the Greek ships had appeared, seized the archbishop and the primates, whom they still held as hostages in the fort; and, as the peasants could not stir, the fleet sailed away without effecting anything.

Our friend went on to relate minutely the trials of those ten days; he named those who had been seized as hostages—all men respected and beloved—and he described with emotion the terror which their arrest had spread all over the island. For the massacres at Constantinople were already known, and the seizure of hostages was considered, reasonably enough, as the prelude to worse sufferings.

We now understood why the town was desolate and gloomy; and at the same time we concluded Smyrna was not the only dangerous residence; but that wherever armed Turks and enslaved Christians were to be found together, there must also exist brutal ferocity on the one hand, and unceasing agony on the other.

We hastened in silence towards our house. When my father knocked at the door a tear trickled down his face; but I felt my heart convulsed with a rapturous flood of old reminiscences; and when Adriana, the orphan daughter of my old nurse, the cheerful playmate of my early childhood, the devoted maid of my mother—when she opened the door and saw us unexpectedly, before her, she stood aghast with amazement and joy. She was on the point of announcing our arrival, when I rushed upon her, and before she had time to utter a word, with one hand I closed her mouth, and with the other I pulled the loose end of her Chiote head-dress. Her tresses fell down loosened, and the white kerchief remained in my grasp. I forgot, at that moment, both the respect due to my father, the seven years that had elapsed during my absence, and the sad auguries under which I returned to my father's house.

My mother's joy when she saw us overpowered all other thoughts. I found her more aged than I remembered her—my dear old mother; and my sisters, whom I had left as little children, were now blooming damsels. Oh, with what joy does a man return, after a lengthened absence, to the home where he was born, and again find himself near those whom he has loved from childhood. How sweet are the first hours of such meeting: the endearments of a beloved mother, when she leads back her son to his old room, where for years past he has not rested; her incoherent, tender words, and the tears of joy with which those words are interrupted. Poor mother! how much she had still to suffer before closing her eyes!

My father wished we should at once go to our tower in the country; but the aldermen would not permit this. None of the better-to-do families were allowed to leave the town. The Turks, besides those they held in the fort, wished to have us all ready to hand under their sword. In spite of ourselves, therefore, we remained in town, trusting that, one way or another, things would not be long calming down.

No one could then foresee the long continuance of the struggle; and I must confess that we at Chio had at first no great hopes of ultimate success. On the contrary, we saw before us the magnitude of the Turkish power, and we judged of it under the influence of old ideas, and under the impressions of terror. Besides, the revolution itself had not yet displayed its strength by its victories on land, and its achievements on the seas. But even later, when the Greek arms began to triumph, the news of their success did not suffice to neutralise the discouragement which the disasters around us sowed in our hearts. For each heroic deed of the insurgents soon received its counter blow wherever the Turks held sway. The first burning of a Turkish line of battle ship was followed by the wail which rose from Cydonia, and the frightful massacres of Smyrna: the defeat of the enemy at Samos was succeeded by the bloody orgies of Cyprus; and the storming of Tripolitza was answered by the devastation of Cassandra.

In the meantime, the archbishop and the primates were detained in the fortress, the garrison of which was daily recruited by fresh arrivals. Oppression increased; the Turks eyed us savagely, while they ostentatiously sharpened their swords; and all along the opposite coast of Asia Minor hordes of savages were amassed, ready to fall upon our unhappy isle. Surely the atmosphere around us was not calculated to raise our spirits. Our heads were bent low before the whirlwind of adversity, and manly hopes found no place in our hearts.

My father's only hope—the hope not of shaking off the yoke, but of bringing about conciliation and compromise—was based on help from Christendom. But his friend Zenakis in no way admitted the probability of such help. My heart sank within me when I heard him deplore the movement, and lament in advance all its consequences. My father seemed unconvinced, and persisted in hopes; but then Zenakis was Vice-Consul —I do not quite remember of which of the secondary Powers—Holland, if I am not mistaken; so that his words were to me full of weight and authority.

Being an old friend of my father's, and a neighbour, he was one of the few who at that time frequented us. Owing to his official position, he was in daily intercourse with the other consuls, and consequently the anti-Hellenic policy of the Powers, which shaped the notions of the Consular body at Chio, was reflected in the language held by

Zenakis. His expressions were neither eulogistic of the present nor encouraging for the future of the revolution.

"Europe, you may rest assured, will not interfere," he repeated again and again to my father. "Kings will have nothing to do with rebels."

"And will they allow the Sultan to butcher every Greek?" cried my father.

"Let them submit to the Sultan, and let them ask for grace;" replied Zenakis. And I fancy I can still hear him wind up with his usual denunciation, whenever the insurgents were mentioned: "The ruin of the nation rests on their souls!"

So the summer passed on, autumn was soon over, and winter succeeded to autumn. Ten months went by, during which we existed as between the hammer and the anvil, forgetting the sorrows of yesterday in the expectation of the morrow.

Reader, have you ever tried the ascent of a high mountain? You begin to climb up with a will; the ascent is a hard task, and sweat soon bathes your brow; yet the nearness of the end lightens the sense of fatigue. You see the summit above you, and you make for it; you approach; but a few steps more and you have reached it. But, no! that was not the top. A projecting curve in the mountain deceived you. The true summit is a short way higher up. The distance does not appear great: forward! And you begin climbing afresh, with knees less firm, with quicker pulsations of the heart. You reach the spot, and you see the summit still farther off. Your powers are already exhausted in the struggle to attain an end which moves off gradually as you think you have touched it. Prostrate and panting, you see at last the sky behind the last peak, and then, dropping on the ground in order to regain strength, you gaze on the valley below you, and you marvel at the height to which you have climbed.

Even so did those months pass on. We ascended the mountain; but from the very outset clouds covered the summit, which we did not see. And when at length we got there, it was only to find a cliff and a precipice at our feet; and instead of resting on the height, we were engulfed into the abyss before us.

So long as the Turks did not massacre and did not make slaves of us, we considered ourselves fortunate, seeing what occurred elsewhere. The women did not leave the house at all, and we ourselves avoided as much as possible all contact with the Turks; we lived stealthily, so to say, and waited patiently, but in great agony, till the wrath of the Lord had passed away.

However, the continued detention of the hostages, the steady increase of the numbers of Asiatic Turks in the fortress, the forcible disarmament of the inhabitants of the island, all this boded no good to us. Of the surrounding islands, Psara on the one side, and Samos on the other, were already free. Attempts at insurrection were made at Mitylene, and the Greek ships, triumphantly scouring the seas, cruised more and more frequently in the waters of Chio.

One evening Zenakis mysteriously brought us the news that the Pacha suspected that an attack on the island was impending. Next day forty more notables were invited into the fortress, and there detained, so that the number of hostages was now doubled. Fortunately my father was not of the wealthiest citizens of Chio, and was therefore not included in the list.

A few days later it was whispered that Samiot ships had disembarked on our islands emissaries, who were hiding in the remoter villages. The Turks were evidently troubled; patrols marched through the villages, and some of the hostages were sent to Constantinople. Things appeared to become menacing, and we foresaw that a crisis was impending.

Our fears were not long in being realised. Towards the afternoon of the 9th of March (1822) some forty ships made their appearance on the sea opposite, and the alarm that the insurgents were down upon us spread from house to house. From the terrace on the top of our house I saw the ships closing upon the harbour, and heard the beating of drums in the fort as a signal of danger. The Turks shut themselves up and awaited the assault.

That same evening, towards sunset, we started for our tower in the country. Nor were we the only fugitives. In presence of imminent danger both the prohibition of the aldermen and the fear of the Turkish authorities had disappeared.

Thus we abandoned our home. Thirty years afterwards I visited my native island as a stranger, and I saw Chio desolate and our house in ruins. But my father died a homeless exile, nor had he the consolation to see his children restored to ease and happiness, even in a foreign land. He died while the distress of ruin and the sorrow of exile still lasted. When we fled, we could not foresee that we abandoned our home for ever, and that we should have to undergo all we afterwards suffered.

The farther we got from the town the

more peasants we met speeding towards it *en masse*. They were unarmed, but they were to receive arms from the fleet. They were evidently informed of what we had remained in ignorance of. Logothetis and Bournias, at the head of three thousand Samiots, were on board the ships, and came to liberate Chio. Unfortunately they brought us not liberty but devastation.

However, they landed next day, and without firing a shot they became masters of the town, hoping that the Turks in the fort would soon be compelled to surrender.

During these events we remained quiet in the country. The booming of guns alone occasionally disturbed our quietness, and reminded us that we reposed on a volcano. Yet the firing was not continuous, and, as for myself, I know not how and for what reason, but there, in the country, I forgot all cares and fears. Was it because I had become accustomed to that existence of continual uneasiness? Was I emboldened by the thought that the flag of liberty waved over my country? Or was it but the vivifying influence of spring and the mysterious charm of resuscitating nature which pervaded me, and thus made me live as the flowers and think as little as the birds of the air? I cannot say; but as often as I revert to that unfortunately short period of our sojourn in our tower, I can bring back to my mind no terrors, no anxieties, no sleepless nights, no days full of suffering. I remember only the orange trees white with blossoms, the air full of perfumes, the songs of the birds, and the creaking of the wooden wheel over our well as it went slowly round. And I can even see before me our old gardener hard at work, and the view from our balcony over the plain, and the sea beyond. That is all I remember.

And yet I was then a young man of one-and-twenty. Now, while I write of these recollections, I am amazed, and I revolt against myself, that instead of taking refuge in our tower with my old parents and my sisters, I did not hasten to seek a place under our flag in the struggle; that I did not take up arms, were it even that I might fall in battle. But now I think and feel differently. Then . . . .

While thus narrating the ups and downs of my life, I owe it to you, my good reader, to make you more familiar with my own humble self. It is necessary I should confess to you in all sincerity and humility why and wherefore I was neither morally nor physically fit to act then as I should now expect that my children would act under similar circumstances. This confession will not exalt me in your eyes, but my intention is not to mislead you, by making myself appear better than I was or am now.

I said both morally and physically. The sad truth is that I am weakly in body, and I have never been able to forget, in the presence of either men or women, the smallness of my stature; being conscious of it, I labour constantly under the impression that others also remark it. Even now, although I enjoy the consideration of my fellow-countrymen, although I often preside at their meetings,—perhaps because only of my advanced age, or because of their kindness towards me,—I confess I can never get the better of the constraint which the sense of my diminutiveness begets within me. And, after all, I am now in good health; but, until I grew up into manhood, the infirmity of my constitution rendered my bodily appearance still more insignificant. Besides, boys were not then reared up as they are now. Neither at school nor afterwards had I any opportunity for bodily exercise. Parents then knew little of the necessity for muscular development of their children, and cared less about it.

Thus, being small in stature and feeble, while in Pappa Flouti's school I had become the butt of my schoolfellows' jokes, and later, in the khan at Smyrna, I passed by the nickname of Loukis the Mite. All this, coupled with my own humble appreciation of my powers, was surely not calculated to develop within me a heroic turn of mind.

Had I known then as much as I do now,

the latent yearnings of my soul might perhaps have sought and found an outlet, and have got the better of my natural shortcomings. But my mind was then as shrunk and as undeveloped as my body. I was very ignorant and unenlightened. Not even orthography had that good old Pappa Floutis succeeded in imparting to me, though he professed to have indoctrinated me in the fables of Æsop, and to have lectured on some of the sermons of the Fathers. The little Italian and French I knew I had picked up in my *Telemachus*, which, by the way, I did not quite read through; and after leaving school I never opened any book but our ledger. I had some vague and confused notions about Leonidas and Marathon, and about the French Revolution. But as to liberty, and independence, and the higher destinies of man, I neither thought anything of, nor had I any clear and definite conception respecting them.

The khan was my world, and a good balance-sheet my patriotism. It was necessary for me to have been sunk in misery, to have seen the destitution and the sufferings of those around me, to have witnessed the throes attending the regeneration of Greece, to have realised the sacrifices and have appreciated the high motives of the death-struggle of her sons, before the eyes of my soul could be opened, and before the fire of patriotism, latent within me, could have burnt into flame. It was only then I felt a thirst for knowledge, that I understood the world, and that I became a man. Alas! still but a small man!

III.

Our tower, and the grounds around it, came into our possession as my mother's marriage portion. Her family possessed of old in that part of the island large estates, which by succession and marriage settlements were subdivided with each generation, but did not go out of the family; so that we were surrounded by my mother's relatives, whose towers lay within easy reach of ours.

There was hardly one of these country seats untenanted at that time. The owners of some lived there all the year round, and others had abandoned their town houses on the same day we had fled, at the approach of the Samiotes. We were therefore in good company; and we appreciated the possibility of seeing our relatives all the more, as, during the reign of terror under which we had existed in town, especially of late, we neither left our houses nor exchanged visits. We kept our doors shut, and the windows only partially open. I search in my mind whether for months together I had seen any stranger ascend our stairs, and I can only recollect Zenani's demure countenance.

We met mostly at our rustic chapel, and when service was over we all assembled in the little garden around the church. Lenttide had again come round, and often under the shadow of the trees there I thought of the emotions with which, on the previous year, my father and I attended liturgy at Saint Photini, after creeping in fear and trembling through the streets of Smyrna.

The little chapel had been built by my mother's great-grandfather, who, in his old age, became a monk. The building still exists, but it is tottering into ruin, and is denuded of everything. The icons, the ornaments, the vestments, the sacred vessels, were all pillaged and destroyed by the Turks. Then, it rose gracefully from amid the trees around, and everything in it was trim and orderly. A small narthex, open in front, formed the entrance; and under cover of this projection a marble seat was placed at each side of the gate. There I often sat, reading the epitaphs engraved on the tombstones with which the narthex was flagged. From the founder downwards most of my mother's relatives had been buried there. In that chapel had my parents been married; and it was their wish to be buried there, under the flags of the narthex, the one next the other. But neither they repose there, nor will my body return to earth in that beloved corner of my native isle. We now live and die dispersed, vagrant in life, exiles in death itself, and the whirlwind which has sown us broadcast has shaken and loosened the sacred bonds which attach the hearts of children to their ancestral resting-places. But as we grow old, . . . I, at least, as I feel the hour of repose approaching, I grieve to think that when my children shall have reached my old age they will not be able to soothe their wearied mind either with the traditions of a home owned by successive generations, or with the reminiscences of the bit of land where their fathers slumber clustered together. When I was young I little considered these things. But my soul now reverts to the past with increasing fondness, and lives upon recollections of old.

To resume my tale. On Thursday morning of the Passion Week we went to the liturgy, and we communed of the Holy Sacrament. It was a magnificent spring morning when we returned from church, and instead of remaining indoors I went on the balcony to eat my Lenten breakfast. But on opening the door upon the balcony, and raising my eyes to the sea beyond, I was stupefied with the sight before me. I left my breakfast there, and ran to call my father, who followed me on the balcony, and we both gazed on the sea before us.

A long line of great ships made for the harbour. They were still distant, but the atmosphere was limpid, and we could make out distinctly the sails bulging out before the wind, and the double and treble white lines on the black hulls of the ships. While these seemed to approach, another line of small craft, their triangular sails catching the wind aside, fled creeping along the coast in the direction of Samos. But the larger vessels, as if hesitating, instead of continuing their course towards the port, suddenly veered round. For an instant I fancied they would put about; but no, they are not retracing their steps; they are tacking in front of Chio, whilst the small ships, still flying to our right, disappear one after the other behind the extreme point of the island.

It was not difficult to understand what was taking place. The Turkish fleet was bearing down in great strength, and the insurgents beat a retreat. But we Chiotes— what would become of us?

I know not how long my father and I remained on the balcony silent and motionless, with our eyes transfixed on the sea.

"Let us fly, let us fly," said he, suddenly turning towards the house. I followed him; and I then saw my mother, with my sisters and Adriana, standing by us on the balcony, and gazing mutely on the sight before us.

My father left the house immediately, and I went after him, by his orders. He wished to consult with our relatives as to what was to be done. We had hardly stepped out of our garden gate when we saw Calanis, my mother's cousin, coming towards us, holding his little daughter by the hand. A few months before he had lost his wife, and his very life now seemed concentrated on love for his orphan child. He was inseparable from her. The graceful form of the child, then in its eleventh year, and the sad expression of its tender features, had won all my sympathies from the very first day of our sojourn in the country.

Calanis was coming to meet my father with the same object which guided our steps.

We now all turned towards the chapel; they went first, talking together; I followed a few steps behind, holding little Despina by the hand. Gazing on the golden locks of her innocent head, I thought of the ships I saw from the balcony, and I recollected with a shudder all I had heard of the doings of the Turks at Smyrna and Cydoniæ.

I walked on silent and full of sadness. Despina said nothing, but I felt her little fingers tremble within my hand. I could see she was frightened; but not knowing what to say in order to cheer her, I stooped and kissed her hand. She then turned her blue eyes towards me, and said, in a trembling voice:

"Louki, will the Turks kill us?"

"No, Despina, my child; we shall go. Be not afraid; no one will harm us."

"They will kill my father. I know they will. They will kill him!"

And she began crying bitterly, but silently. The tears streamed down her little face, and she repeated:

"They will kill him. The Turks kill. They will kill my father!"

"Don't cry, Despina; don't be afraid."

I wished to console her, but I had no words, and the bitterness of her wail choked my voice.

Most of our neighbours had already collected in the narthex of the chapel. We also sat on the marble seats. Calanis took the child on his knees, and the older men began to consult.

They were not long in making up their minds. It was manifest that there were no means sufficient to offer opposition, and that the Turks would soon be masters of the island. We all knew *a priori* how the Turks treat conquered countries. It was therefore resolved that we should move to the western part of the island, and there disperse, wherever we could each find refuge. We thus avoided the Turks, and approached the coast opposite Psara, whence we hoped to be rescued. With aching hearts we bade each other good-bye, we gave a last kiss to the icons, and we separated.

From that day I never saw our little chapel again.

On our way home, my father told me that he intended seeking, for a few days, the hospitality of his two old uncles, who lived on their farm. It lay on the other side of the hill which shut in our valley. As soon as we got back, he ordered the gardener to load two mules with bedding and provisions, and to go in advance to inform the old gentlemen of our arrival, and there wait with the mules.

The gardener having set off, my father called me into the room where he had been closeted with my mother. I found them filling a sack with plate and other valuables; another sack lay on the sofa already filled. The second one having also been tied up, my father lifted it on his back, and bade me take hold of the other. My mother opened for us the door, and we left the room, he first, and I following, each carrying his sack, until we reached the most outlying part of the garden, near a thicket of trees. I laid down my load and brought two spades. There, under the shade of an old apple-tree by the well, at a place which at my father's bidding I noted and accurately impressed upon my mind, we both set to work digging a trench. In it we placed the two sacks, the one on top of the other, we covered them up, pressed down the earth, and levelled the surface; and, making sure we had not been observed, we turned back.

"Do not forget this reserve," said my father; "if I die, you will be the protector of your mother and sisters."

Outside the gate of the house four asses were standing ready to start, and Adriana was hurrying on our departure. My father and mother and my sisters mounted on the asses and we started, Adriana and I bringing up the rear on foot.

That very instant the distant thunder of a gun was suddenly heard, and it was soon followed by closer firing. We looked at each other in silence. The roar of artillery was steadily kept up. The Turks at the fort and from the ships had begun to celebrate the advent of their horrible triumph.

"Woe to Chio!" cried my father; and we hurried on.

The farm to which we were bound was situated in a defile, so that its view was confined, and the sea could not thence be seen. There my father's old uncles lived in undisturbed retirement. The older of the two was a man of great sagacity and experience, and had spent many years of his life trading at Amsterdam. He had there become acquainted with Coray, then also engaged in commercial pursuits, and had since kept up with that learned man an occasional but most friendly correspondence; for my uncle also gave some of his time to literature. All this invested him with a certain weight in the eyes of his countrymen. Men of letters were then more seldom to be met with, and consequently were held in greater esteem, of which indeed they were worthy. They knew thoroughly what they professed to know, and laboured with self-denial for the enlightenment of our people.

I had not seen my uncle since my early

childhood; but I thought of him always with respect; and our short sojourn near him on that occasion increased my appreciation of his wisdom and his many virtues. He foretold us all that Chio was about to suffer—the massacres, the pillage, the captivity, the exile, the dispersion; in a word, all that took place. On the whole, he condemned the insurrection as premature, and the future seemed to him black and cheerless. But then he was very old, and in his retirement he nourished his mind with the cold dictates of experience and the contents of books. Would revolutions ever take place in any country, if the audacity and inexperience of youth were wanting? Old men naturally incline to inaction or postponement; they counsel patience and circumspection. I feel this myself, and I know it from my own experience now.

The other brother was deaf, and spoke but rarely. Downcast and melancholy, he seemed a stranger to the things of this world, his only amusement and occupation being wood carving. I have still a small specimen of his handiwork, representing the Annunciation, which he gave me then.

My parents in vain urged the two old men to flee with us. The deaf brother shook his head in sign of refusal. The other said—"The life still left us is but short; why should we take pains to prolong it? You have duties towards your children: you go."

And so they remained in their tower. No one knows what their fate was. Neither they, nor their old servant, nor the gardener and his family, have ever been seen or heard of since. God only knows in what slave-market the gardener and his children were sold, and on what Turkish estate they slaved their existence away. As for the old men, especially the deaf one, they had no marketable value. Who would buy them, and for what purpose? Such captives were not bartered; they were butchered. May their agony have been short! At least, they were not married, and there were no widows and orphans to mourn over them. But we preserved the memory of the good old men in fond respect; and even now, after the lapse of so many years, my heart sinks within me while I write of them.

We remained there four days only, during which time we were daily informed by the peasants of what took place in the island.

Even before the fleet cast anchor, the Turks from the fort had thrown themselves upon the town, and begun to pillage and massacre. When, during our flight, we had heard the firing of guns, the crews of the ships were landing to swell the number of executioners. Next day the sea was covered with small craft bringing over from the opposite coast the savage hordes who had so long been lying in wait for their prey. Then horror reached its height. The town did not suffice to quench their pent up fury, and they were let loose on the surrounding country. On Easter Sunday the terrible holocaust of Saint Minas took place. All resistance had now ceased; such of the insurgents as had not fled had been scattered and were in hiding. Nothing impeded the advance of the wild beasts but the glut of ready victims; and in proportion as these were exhausted, the circle of devastation extended, so that we could hear the Turks approach nearer and nearer to our place of refuge.

Hear them approach, did I say? It is but an abstract and cold expression. But how can I adequately describe the horror of these events? It is for you, reader, to supplement the insufficiency of my narrative by imparting life into the scenes, and by vivifying the impressions which my memory now reflects. It is one thing to read, comfortably seated in your room, of devastations in a distant or unknown country, and at a bygone time, and another thing to hear that your acquaintances, and your relatives, and friends, and countrymen, are massacred or carried into slavery; that homes familiar to you, and which you visited but the other day, are burnt and pillaged. It is a widely different thing to be told by name that such and such a friend has been killed and his wife made a slave; that she was seen dragged along by a savage Turk, wailing, and in despair. You know her voice; you have heard her often talk to you merrily, and you fancy that you now listen to her rending, piteous screams, that you see her, with upturned head and dishevelled hair, being led into captivity, into shame. And you think of her husband and her children! You are yourself near at hand, with your aged mother and your virgin sisters, and you expect, from one moment to another, to see her iniquitous persecutors appear before you. Ah! may God spare you such experience!

Information of such events reached us in uninterrupted succession, so much so that we grew callous to the enormity of the disaster. We became almost brutalised by constant fear. It was actually by force that my uncle induced my father to fly.

We therefore loaded our mules again with our bedding and with provisions, and sent the gardener in advance, with instructions to wait for us at the village of St. George, in the westerly part of the island, where my father recollected he had a rustic friend, to whose child he had stood godfather. Bidding farewell to our old uncles, we followed shortly afterwards, and reached St. George towards the afternoon, exhausted by the heat and the fatigue of the journey.

On entering the village we saw something unusual had happened. Everyone was astir, the streets were full of people, and amongst them were some armed men, who appeared to be strangers. Women and children stood at every door, looking on and talking excitedly. One would have thought it was a feast-day; indeed, it was then holiday time, but the anxiety marked on every face betokened that the village was not in a festive mood.

My father approached an old villager who stood in the open doorway of his cottage, and inquired as to the whereabouts of his friend. He was no longer in the village; he had left it a year ago. My father asked again whether our gardener had arrived, but neither gardener nor mules had appeared. He then inquired why that stir—whence the armed men. They were Samiotes flying before the Turks, and Logothetis was with them.

Logothetis in the village and the Turks in pursuit! And we had come to St. George to avoid the Turks! And neither our *compère* nor the gardener to be seen; and we, exhausted and famished, without refuge, without guide! The good peasant took pity upon us and ushered us into his cottage. We sat down, waiting for our gardener. Since the morning we had not refreshed ourselves. Our host asked us if we were hungry, and offered us his frugal supper; but my father thanked him, being loth to deprive him of his bread. Still, as hour followed upon hour, and our gardener did not appear, my father sent me to buy what food I could obtain. I had hardly left the cottage, when, in the light of the setting sun, I saw before me a general stampede. Women with children in their arms, men, their hands loaded with chattels, all ran out of the village, exchanging incoherent words, while the armed men, closing their ranks, were making ready to barricade the entrance.

It was like the sudden whirl of the leaves on the ground before the storm bursts out.

"The Turks are upon us. Fly, hide!" cried out to us the old peasant.

We were already outside the cottage, all of us; we had no preparations to make for a flight. I hurriedly untied our asses from the trees where they had been made fast, and, terror-stricken, we ran along with the stream of the fugitives.

We passed the night on the march — whither bound we knew not. But we had walked far and over a difficult country, on a stormy night under a gloomy sky, the moon showing at intervals through the clouds. We were hungry, sleepless, exhausted with fatigue; still we fled. We were often startled, fancying we had heard firing of guns, or shouts, or the thud of horses' feet, and more than once we stopped short in order to lie down and take breath, for we were most of us on foot.

We made up, altogether, a numerous and long convoy, and being afraid lest we should be separated, we endeavoured to keep our own little circle united within that surging crowd.

The morning found us on the sea-shore, at a desert bay opposite the island of Psara. There it was we desired and hoped to take refuge. But the wind was blowing hard, and neither inside the bay nor in the open could we see ship or boat of any sort. The shore was already full of fugitives who had arrived before us, and had collected there in the same hope as that in which we had come. We had not seen or heard anything of them from a distance, but on approaching the beach, we perceived under the olive trees, which reached almost to the sea, human forms lying on the ground in little knots. There these unfortunate people had passed the night, during which, driven on by the tempest, we had marched towards the same point, as to a harbour of refuge.

Our arrival, and the first rays of the rising sun, put in motion that camp of fugitives; and before we got near enough to mix with them, we saw under the olive trees women and children, old men and young, sit up and turn their eyes towards us, whilst some of the crowd came on to see who we were.

We then halted; the women dismounted, and we all sat at the foot of a large tree. Many years have passed away, and much have I since suffered, but never shall I forget the feeling of exhaustion with which I was then overpowered. For twenty-four hours I had been on the march without refreshment or rest. I lay down on the bare earth by the side of my mother, and shut my eyes, feeling no strength in my limbs, and being unable to gather a thought in my head. I felt my mother's hand press on my forehead; I half opened my eyes and saw her dear face bent over me. We exchanged no words, but she stooped and kissed me, and my eyes were again closed.

My father had advanced to meet those who were coming towards us. Presently he returned, followed by an elderly man. I did not know who he was; but my mother recognised him, and getting up she ran towards him. The old man opened his arms and pressed her to his bosom. He was her father's brother.

Up to that moment we had none of us given vent to tears. The fear of impending danger, the constant movement, the rapid succession of scenes and impressions—all this kept our nervous system in tension. We were prostrate in mind and in body, yet our eyes had remained tearless. But now, in the arms of her uncle, my poor mother hid her head in his bosom and abandoned herself to be overpowered by her long pent-up grief. Her sobs and sighs tore my heart. My sisters clung to her and cried, and my father covered his face with his hands, whilst poor Adriana bit her lips, trying to make a show of courage for the sake of the others. As for me, I felt as if my heart rose up within my neck, and my eyes became dim with tears. And there was wailing and lamentation under the olive tree which shaded us.

Our old uncle set my mother on the ground, still sobbing, and went to procure for us some food. He returned with fresh cheese; it was all he could find. For there was not a spare morsel of bread amidst that great host of miserable creatures. With fresh cheese, therefore, we consoled our hunger.

Still there was no vessel to be seen, the violence of the wind did not abate, the sea was high, and we remained exposed on the beach, without cover, without protection of any sort. Were the Turks to arrive, we had no other refuge left us but the waves; and we expected to see them appear from one moment to another. We therefore consulted with my uncle, and it was arranged we should seek shelter in the village of

Mesta, close by, there to bide our time, until, by some possibility, we found means to leave the island.

Thus we were again on the move, and after some hours' march, we reached Mesta in a pitiable condition.

IV.

The villages of Chio, especially in the south of the island, are built like strongholds, and are pent up like prisons. Properly speaking they have no walls, but on the four outer sides the backs of the houses are so connected as to form a continuous bulwark. The doors of the houses face inward on the village, the central street of which, abutting at each end on the outer bulwark, forms the gates. These openings are, in fact, gates, for they are shut in with iron doors.

Such villages always reminded me of our khan at Smyrna, the only difference being that, instead of the great city which encircled our khan, the villages are surrounded by green hills; and instead of pale tradesmen, they are peopled with robust peasants; and in lieu of the open courtyard of the khan, narrow passages and closely-built structures crowd the space shut in by the outer four-sided line of houses. In the centre of the village there rises, as a rule, a tower, the entrance into which is so far above the level of the street, that it can only be reached by a wooden ladder, or by a rope. These towers, relics of the Genoese dominion, are the citadels of the villages.

Such was the village of Mesta, where we took refuge. The villagers received us kindly, and placed at our disposal an unoccupied house, the vacant rooms of which we divided between ourselves, my uncle, and two other families, whom common sufferings had now for the first time brought us in contact with.

Our privations were many and various. But who thought then of comforts or of the common necessities of life? The main object was to preserve life, and this was about all our diet could accomplish. Even bread was hard to obtain on all occasions, and our fare consisted generally of figs, beans, carobs, and wild herbs.

Thus the days passed on, amid hopes and fears. As to our projected escape to Psara, we were compelled to abandon all idea of it, the news which reached us thence being very discouraging. The island was already overcrowded with fugitives, and the Psariotes, with hardly sufficient means to maintain them, neither could nor wished to receive new arrivals. Water had already become scarce, and the crowding together of large numbers of destitute refugees had engendered sickness, which seemed to herald a still more fearful pestilence. They therefore sent word to Chio, recommending that fugitives should be directed to other islands of the Ægean, and offering readily for that purpose their ships and their men.

But at Mesta we began to hope that there would be no longer any need of escape. Two weeks had now elapsed since the arrival of the Turkish fleet. The insurgents had left the island, or were hiding, scattered in the interior, whilst the peaceable inhabitants of the town, and most of the villagers, had neither risen against the Turkish authorities, nor had they been implicated in the revolutionary movement. Why, then, should persecutions continue? Why should terror be perpetuated, when all possibility of resistance had disappeared? Were the innocent victims already sacrificed not sufficient? Was the outburst of Turkish fury not adequately satiated? Thus cogitating, we expected from day to day the proclamation of an amnesty, and leave to return to our homes.

And, in fact, the violence of the Turks had diminished perceptibly. We heard less firing, and fewer murders and hangings were reported; it was even rumoured that the consuls were mediating for a free pardon in favour of the rayahs, and that the Pacha seemed disposed to clemency. Such rumours reached us and raised our hopes.

On the ninth day of our sojourn at Mesta,

we really thought that our woes were drawing to an end. Two of the consuls came to the village with olive branches in their hands, bringing tidings of comfort. They presented to us a petition to sign, promising that on our making an act of submission the Pacha would pardon us.

Pardon us! and for what? We were no insurgents; we had harmed no one; we had pillaged no man's property; we had dishonoured no woman; nor had we murdered or made slaves of any. What, then, were we to be pardoned for?

But these are my thoughts now. Then we did not reason thus; the very hope of being rescued from that unbearable existence was a source of true joy for us. We therefore signed readily, all of us, old and young, without so much as inquiring as to the contents of the document; we signed with both hands, calling for blessings upon the good consuls who had mediated. We now breathed freely, confident that persecution had ceased, and that we could return to our homes unmolested.

But should we find our homes as we left them? After the eruption of the Samiotes and the peasants under Burnias, after the violent cannonading from the fort and the fleet, especially after the unrestrained pillage by the Turks, we could entertain but little hope of this. Still the longing to return took possession of us all at Mesta. We wished to see our homes again, no matter in what condition; and the fear lest we should find them destroyed rather increased than checked that desire.

Such is man! Whatever he loves, he clings to the more as the danger of losing it increases. And when the loss is irretrievable, and hope has vanished, it is then that the widowed heart realises the degree of the love it cherished. Thus we linger in churchyards, and sit on the stones which cover the remains of our beloved departed ones. Thus, after a fire which has destroyed whole quarters, we see men roam over the still smoking ruins, seeking traces of their homes, and gazing for hours on the spot where their house once stood, and on the stones which formed its walls.

The promises of the consuls had so elated our hopes, that we wished to return at once. But the older men amongst us restrained our impatience, suspecting lest the proffered amnesty should be an artifice of the Turks, calculated to deceive the consuls, and a trap wherewith the more easily to lure us to destruction. They had a greater experience of Turkish character; but the rest of us confidently relied on the promises and the protection of the consuls. After some consideration and debate, and with a certain amount of hesitation, it was at length resolved that some of us younger men should go on as scouts, and that the others should wait at Mesta for news from us, or our return.

Early next morning I started with two other young men of my age. There is no need to mention their names. To what purpose should I indicate by name in each case those whose ill-luck was linked to mine? Of my two companions, the one, now a happy old gentleman, holds a high position in one of the Greek communities abroad. Often have we since met and talked of days gone by and of our common sufferings. The other, who was spared then, died shortly afterwards at Tinos. Many who had escaped the clutches of the Turks were thus mown down by death. Exhausted by long privations and troubles, many who had fled before the enemy's sword fell afterwards premature victims to disease.

Well, then, we took leave of our friends at Mesta, and set off, the three of us, for the town. The impressions of recent disasters were still fresh upon our minds, and we were not free from apprehension lest we should fall in with armed Turks, who might be ignorant of or indifferent to the better dispositions of the Pacha.

But we were all still young, the morning breeze had an invigorating effect upon us, and the mastic-covered hills around Mesta gave forth a health-imparting aroma. Gradually, therefore, hope dispelled our fears, and we walked on with a lighter step, cheering our march with pleasant conversation. But neither our cheerfulness nor our journey was to continue long.

We now saw at a distance the village of Elata, where we purposed to rest after our walk, and to obtain information for our journey farther on. The sun was scorching, and we quickened our steps towards the white-washed houses of the village.

We had reached the outskirts, when suddenly we heard wailing and loud cries of women. We all three stood still and looked at each other. Were the Turks in the village? Such was our first thought. We listened, and the cries continued; they were clearly the lamentations of women. Guided by the sound, we traversed the deserted streets of the village, and soon arrived in front of the church.

There the villagers were gathered in a crowd; and, lifted above their heads, we saw two hearses, which were being carried into the church, the one after the other. Around them pressed the women, crying and wailing pitifully.

The funeral procession having entered the church, I asked one of the peasants who were the two dead. He said, with tears in his eyes, that a band of Turks having met that morning three young men outside the village, fired at them and went their way. Of the three, one escaped unhurt, and running back to the village, gave the alarm. The bodies of the other two had been brought in a short while ago.

What, then, of the assurances of security? What hope was there of our sufferings coming to an end? Our elders were right. Those two corpses, and the lamentations of the women, were the proofs of Turkish good faith, the guarantees of Turkish clemency.

We returned to Mesta quicker than we had come from it, and minus our previous cheerfulness. They were amazed to see us return; but our narrative of the scene at Elata filled them with consternation, and the pre-existing distress of mind at once superseded the hopes which had hardly taken root.

My father was the only one who persisted in his illusions. The encounter was a mere accident; the decision of the Pacha could not yet have been known; besides, even those Turks did not remain at Elata, so that their firing at the young men was no proof of the resumption of systematic persecutions; things would surely settle down. Thus he reasoned; but the experience of the past filled the rest of us with fear, and deprived us of all confidence in the vaunted good intentions of the Pacha.

"Let us go, let us fly," said the women; their children cried, and I could not dismiss from my mind the sight of those two hearses at the entrance of the church, nor the wail of the women lamenting their dead.

That same day my mother's uncle, by dint of liberal rewards and still more generous promises, succeeded in inducing a young peasant to carry, by any possible means, a letter to Psara. He begged his friends there to provide us with means of escape. "Let a vessel once approach," said he to my father, "and you may remain here if you choose. But let it only come in time."

My father remained silent, and seemed hesitating. Was he afraid of the dangers of the flight and the bitterness of exile, or did he confide in the mediation of the consuls, and think that by hiding in the meantime on our own island we might weather the storm with greater safety? Or again, had he, under the weight of so many successive emotions, lost all self-reliance, and was now in doubt what to choose and how to decide?

Next morning we were all gathered in the ground-floor entrance of the house, which served as a common room. Sitting on the door-steps and on the staircase, we were, as usual, discussing what was to be done; we awaited what the day would bring forth, calculating when we might reasonably expect an answer from Psara. Adriana alone was absent. She had gone to procure for us provisions. She had more than once succeeded in varying our poor fare by gathering wild herbs from the surrounding hills. As, however, she was long returning, my mother felt uneasy, and repeatedly opened the door and looked out into the street to see if she would appear.

Adriana was a veritable Providence—the general support of our unfortunate party at Mesta. Full of self-denial and devotion, she looked after my mother and sisters, and saw to the wants of us all. She found time for everything, and nothing escaped her attention. It was she who procured or invented our daily fare; it was she who brought water from the well. She had succeeded, by means of straw and some old carpets, in extemporising beds for all of us in the vacant rooms of that house. And, having struck up friendship with the peasants, she inquired into and ascertained all that was going on, and brought us information from outside. Her activity was inexhaustible and her good humour unalterable. Her heart was as robust and her mind as healthy as her physique was perfect, and often, by her vivacity and cheerfulness, she contrived to bring back smiles on our lips in the midst of that general gloom.

The day advanced, however, and my mother's anxiety increased. I did not wish to add to it by expressing my misgivings, but I was as apprehensive as the rest of us seemed to be getting. What had become of her? Why so late? Such were our constant remarks, when the door was flung open, and Adriana appeared pale as death, trembling, her hair dishevelled, her dress torn, and her breast uncovered and bloodstained. Her whole appearance bespoke a fearful struggle, terror, and shame.

My mother jumped up, covered her eyes with her hands, and shrieked with horror: "Ah! the Turks! the Turks!" and, seizing her daughters, drew them close within her embrace.

Adriana, the one hand on the open door, pointed with the other towards the street, and, panting for breath, she could hardly articulate the words she endeavoured to pronounce: "Fly, hide!"

In an instant we were all of us in the street with Adriana.

Whither were we going? What doing? An instinctive impulse guided our steps in a direction contrary to the entrance of the village. We were trying to escape the Turks, and we did not consider that by running away from the entrance we shut ourselves up in the village. But who reasons in such moments?

While we were thus flying terror-stricken and confused, not knowing where to take refuge, an old woman standing by the door of a humble cottage saw us, and, taking pity upon us, extended to us her hand. "Come in, good Christians," said she; "let me hide you here."

We all rushed in through the open door, following the good old woman. Providence had inspired her. To her we owe our preservation—our very existence. I never saw her since, I do not even know her name, but

I have never forgotten her good-natured face, nor have I ever ceased to bless her memory. May the Almighty have rewarded her, and have let her repose in peace!

At the back of the cottage there was an open yard, with a stable at the end. In that stable she hid us. Her cows were out grazing in the fields, and they did not return either that evening or on the following nights, but left us in undisputed possession of their abode. The Turks did not capture women and children only. Anything they could lay hands upon was good plunder; but that time we were not the sufferers by the robbery of the cows of the poor old widow.

The entrance into the stable was a narrow and dark passage, but the stable itself extended into a considerable quadrangle, without windows or any other opening, so that when the door of the passage was closed upon the yard the darkness inside was thick, and to the stench inside there was no outlet. Four days and nights were we, eighteen souls in all, pent up within that dungeon.

On the evening of the first day the good woman brought us a bag full of figs, and when our eyes became somewhat accustomed to the darkness, we discovered, in a corner of the stable, a can with some water in it, intended for the cows. Thanks to those figs and that water we did not die of inanition. As for bedding, we found on a shelf, projecting from one of the sides of the stable, a quantity of straw, which we spread on the ground, so that the women and children might not lie on the filthy soil.

From our hiding-place we often heard, sometimes near and again from afar, the howling of the Turks and the groans of the Christians. The last night of our sojourn in the stable, especially, we had them only too near us, for they passed that night in the cottage of the old woman, and we could hear distinctly their conversation and the recital of their execrable exploits.

The chief business of these Turks was to discover the fugitives who were hiding. They dispatched the men, and carried away the women and children to the town as slaves. They did not, as a rule, molest the peasants, except so far as insults and beating and kicks went, and the consumption of their provisions. But they never remained long in the same village. One band arrived towards nightfall; they feasted and slept, and next morning began the business of slaughter, captivity, and pillage; the first lot left with their prisoners and booty, and was succeeded by a fresh band in the evening.

So we waited, in the hope that they might feel surfeited with blood, and that, victims running short, persecution might be stayed; and we prayed God we might not be discovered to the end.

How can I describe the agony of those interminable days! We dare not speak, lest the merest sound should betray us. Adriana alone wept unceasingly, and at times sobs escaped her. My father then would impose silence. He said to her—" Do you wish to betray us?"

And Adriana hid her face, and her wailings were not heard. My mother went up to her to caress and console her.

"Do not touch me," she said to her; "do not touch me; you will taint your hands."

Miserable girl! Her black despair in that dark and filthy refuge was the most terrible warning of the fate which awaited the rest of the women were the Turks to discover us.

The last night we remained awake with the almost certain fear that we should not escape their grip. The door of the stable but just separated us from them. In the morning silence reigned in the cottage, but the village was in commotion. How slowly those hours passed! Would the Turks return again near us? Should we have them there another night? We all felt as if we could no longer bear it.

Towards evening we heard them in the yard preparing for departure, and we stood breathless, awaiting their hoped-for disappearance. Suddenly the husky voice of a Turk thundered out:

"But let us just see, before we go, what there is in this shed."

I made the sign of the cross, and a cold sweat came over me.

The door of the stable creaked loudly as it was flung open, and revealed the terrible form of a Turk. With one hand he held a naked sword; with the other a stick, at the end of which hung a lamp. Its glimmer lit up the face of the Turk, and behind him appeared the heads of more Turks, eyeing inquisitively the darkness before them. I was sitting down at the far end of the stable, opposite the door.

If I live for a thousand years I shall never forget that appalling apparition. We had almost ceased breathing. The Turk put out his foot, and made a step forward. A loud splash of the water into which he stepped echoed through the barn, and drew from the Turk a frightful oath.

"There is nothing but filth in here," he added. "Let us go."

The door was swung back with a crash, and

they departed. We were saved! A whisper, an involuntary sigh, might have betrayed us all. But God took pity upon us, and it was His will we should be saved.

Our escape then appeared to us as a good omen for the future, and we waited with renewed fortitude the end of our trials.

Indeed, our hopes were not vain. That same evening at nightfall the door of the barn was again opened—this time, however, by a friend, our peasant messenger, whom my uncle had sent to procure for us a vessel. By what means he had accomplished his errand, how he discovered our hiding-place, I know not. But he brought us tidings that a Psariot ship waited for us at a lonely creek not far from the village, and he was ready to conduct us there at once.

The darkness of the night, the fear of the Turks, the uncertainty of the future, the dangers of the flight, the recollection of our previous fruitless wanderings, all this caused us many hesitations at that moment. Yet, if we remained there, our doom on the morrow or the next day was certain; whereas we might perhaps succeed in saving ourselves if we now fled.

It was therefore decided we should venture it; and we started under the guidance of the peasant. Holding one another by the hand, we arrived silently at the skirt of the village on the side opposite to the entrance. We avoided the gate, fearing lest it was guarded by Turks.

Our guide had well concerted his plans. We entered a deserted house, in order to escape from the back windows. The night was dark, but we could make out the precipitous ground outside. We hung out a rope, and I was the first to descend, tying the rope round my waist, and holding on by the hands, while they lowered me gradually from the top. The other men followed, and took charge of the women and children as they were let down. Last of all our guide jumped down alone, and again taking the lead, he marched us towards the beach.

The distance was not great, but it was no

easy matter walking stealthily at night, exhausted, and surrounded by old men, women, and children, with no clear notion where we were going, and with a constant fear lest the Turks should reappear.

V.

It was early dawn when we reached the heights overlooking the creek, where the means of rescue awaited us. A silver streak of dim light marked the sky, and heralded the rise of the sun.

At the foot of the steep hill on which we halted we could make out the sea and the beach, but not a ripple was to be heard. Inside the creek the sea was perfectly calm. At some distance farther out the peasant pointed out to us the ship. I could not distinguish its hull on the dark waters, but following our guide's outstretched finger, I saw the two masts, which appeared to be moving towards us, with the sails hanging loosely from them. We quickened our steps, and in a few more minutes we stood on the beach.

The good ship had come from Psara not for us alone. The captain had taken care to make his arrival known overnight, and many were the fugitives who flocked from the villages around, and from the caverns where they had been hiding. The beach was already strewn with them when we got there, and more kept on arriving after us.

Fortunately the first comers had given the signal agreed upon, and the vessel was already moving into the creek, when, from the top of the hill, I made out its masts. As we got near the groups of fugitives, we saw that the eyes of all were turned towards the sea. The boat was coming. It approached. We could hear the oars dip into the sea, and the rowlocks labour under the pressure of each stroke. And standing there on the beach, we bent our ears in silence, intent upon catching those comforting sounds as they became more and more distinct.

When, however, the boat arrived alongside, and the sailors leapt on shore, the silence was broken. It was succeeded by a hubbub and confusion, for all were impatient to get on board, and there was much pushing against the rocks; the fugitives were many and the boat small. But the sturdy voice of the coxswain, and the stalwart arms of the sailors, soon restrained the impatience of the crowd.

"Be calm," he cried; "we shall save you all. We shall leave none behind!"

The boat left with its first freight, while the coxswain and three sailors remained on the shore with their arms. As it went to and fro, the number of those on the beach grew smaller; but the impatience of those left behind increased at every journey of the little craft. They grew more impatient as light spread over the horizon. The sun had not yet appeared, but the sea had already begun to assume the colour of day.

About half were already on board, and we still remained on the shore; we saw the boat return, and we prayed that our turn might not be long coming, when a gunshot resounded, and was followed by the whiz of a bullet. All eyes were at once turned towards the heights behind us, and there, to our right, on the top of the hill, we saw in outline the figures of four men.

"Good heavens, the Turks are upon us!"

The terror spread on that beach by the unexpected appearance of our persecutors was indescribable. A second and a third shot followed. The groups of fugitives were scattered, and we all ran to the foot of the hill, seeking protection under projecting rocks. The four sailors alone remained at their post, and lifting up their guns, took deliberate aim, and the four fired simultaneously. The Turks on the hill did not reply to this salute. Was it out of fear, or did the shots take effect, or were they the advance-guard of a more numerous body, and expected reinforcements before falling upon us? And then what would be our fate? What resistance could we offer?

In the meantime the boat was again approaching, and the firing having ceased, we took courage and ran again towards the sea. Should we all escape in time? Would the Turks reappear on the hill? The boat was now alongside the rocks, when I saw my father approach the coxswain and speak to him earnestly, pointing to my sisters and myself, while the brave sailor withdrew his hand, in which my father tried to place some money. At the same time my mother coming from behind, took me by the hand. I turned round.

"My child," she said, "take your sisters, and go with our blessing. Leave us here to the mercy of God."

And so saying, she put in my pocket a small packet containing all the jewels she had managed to save. I threw myself on her neck, embraced her, and cried out, "Never, never! we shall all be saved together."

But my father laid hold of my arm.

"Go with your sisters," said he firmly; "we shall soon follow."

The boat was already full, and in it were seated my sisters. My father pushed me from one side, the coxswain pulled me from the other, and before I had time to expostulate or resist, I found myself in the boat.

The oars were at once put in motion. I turned back to look once more at my mother, when I saw smoke on the top of the hill, and a gun shot was again heard. The crowd on the rocks now began to press close together; those behind pushed forward, and some had already fallen in the sea. All at once I discovered that my mother was amongst them. I don't quite know how I managed to hold out my arm to her from the boat, how she seized it, how another old lady held on with both hands to my mother's frock. But the boat went on, and the two, being towed by me somehow, floated along, until we lifted them out of the water. I do not even recollect clearly how we ever got on board the ship.

In the meantime the firing continued at intervals. Still the boat went to and fro, and each time I scanned her freight from the ship, trying to see if my father and

Adriana were there. It was only on her last journey that I saw them coming.

We were now on board the ship—a hundred and eighty souls in all, as it turned out on our being counted afterwards, and, thank God, the Turks, from the hill, had not succeeded in diminishing our numbers.

The schooner now spread her sails, and began to move under a gentle but favourable breeze. She was still at the entrance of the creek, when we saw the heights around swarm with Turks. The first few were in fact only the advance guard; but, with God's help, the others were too late in coming up, so that we were now safe and sound, and beyond the reach of their murderous weapons.

My adventures in life have been many and various, but I have never been shipwrecked. The sea, so far at least, has treated me kindly. Yet whenever I read descriptions of such disasters, I am reminded of the terrible hours of our flight from Chio. The shipwrecked mariner who from a foundering ship looks upon the distant shore, can surely not experience emotions more anguishing than those we have suffered, with this difference, that we felt sinking during that agony on the beach, and our rock of salvation was the good ship on board of which we were carried in small batches, while the Turks fired at us from the hill.

When at length I saw the schooner move off, and all those who had undergone the same dangers with us safe on board, I felt my heart filled with joy at our salvation. This was my first feeling—a narrow feeling perhaps of egotism. I did not then think of those who remained at Chio; of the many who, less fortunate than ourselves, were hiding in caves and in underground places, still suffering the martyrdom from which we had escaped. No; I confess that at that moment Chio, nay, the whole world, was for me the ship and those in it. Therein were my feelings centred, therein my thoughts confined.

Having now reached the open sea, and a

certain amount of order and quietness having been restored on deck, the fact that I had remained without any food for a long time began to assert itself. This was no new sensation. Often in the course of our recent adventure I had experienced the agony of hunger and thirst. May God spare you, reader, this trial, save when a well-supplied table awaits you. But to be hungry, and to see those around you pale with exhaustion, to know not whence to procure a morsel of bread, to need every available particle of strength in order to minister to the wants of the dear ones around you . . . Well, it is only he who has undergone such privations that can understand their bitterness.

Our kind-hearted captain had not forgotten that we needed food, and ordered biscuits to be served out. It was to us like manna in the desert. We accepted the biscuits, blessing the name of God, and heartily thanked the captain. And soon there was to be heard only the cheerful mutter of so many mouths greedily grinding the hard ship's biscuits.

Adriana alone would not eat. She sat near the quarter-deck, with her elbows resting on her knees, and her face hid in her hands. The captain went up to her and endeavoured to encourage and comfort her. But she remained silent and motionless, and did not even lift up her head. I then put my hand on her shoulder and begged her to look up; but I did not manage to say much; I saw the tears streaming through her fingers, and my voice failed me. My mother sat near us. I pointed with my hand to Adriana, and my mother, understanding my gesture, got up and went to the unfortunate girl. She knelt before her, she lifted her hands from her forehead, dried her tears, and spoke to her words of womanly tenderness and comfort.

I left them, my heart aching with grief. I moved on towards the forecastle, there to look at the sea which our good ship ploughed up, and on the rocks of Psara, appearing just ahead of us. We were approaching the port, and in a short time we were able to see the ships in it, and the town standing above them. In a few more minutes we rode at anchor in the harbour.

Then, for the first time, I gazed upon the heroic little isle, which was doomed to be destroyed like Chio. But Psara had inflicted in the very vitals of Turkey a fearful wound; whereas from Chio there arose but lamentations and sighs. Psara was destroyed, indeed, but only after the torch of Canaris had lit up in the Greek seas an immortal fire.

We were not allowed to land. The Psariotes were afraid lest they should be compelled to receive us, and they could not well afford to house more refugees on the island. The very water which they sent us to quench our thirst before leaving was in these circumstances a sacrifice.

The wind still blew fair, and the captain was anxious we should sail again before it fell. He proposed to land us at Mykonos, because at Tinos there were already many refugees from Smyrna and Chio, and from other towns, and typhus had followed them there; whereas at Mykonos the place was healthy and less crowded. It was therefore decided we should go to Mykonos. What difference did it make to us—Tinos or Mykonos? All we wished for was a harbour of refuge, and a hospitable roof under which to lay our heads. Above all, that there should be no Turks within reach of us.

At about sunset we hoisted the anchor and set sail. During all this time Adriana had remained mute and buried in sadness. Neither our arrival at Psara, nor our departure thence, nor the general movement and the hubbub on board ship, availed to stir her from the lethargy into which she had plunged. Everything appeared to be strange to her. Her eyes were fixed, but one could see her gaze was blank. An indescribable sadness was depicted in her look, her attitude, her very silence. When spoken to, she lifted up her eyes slowly, as if she laboured to detach herself from her thoughts, and she replied slowly and with an effort. If my mother took up her hand and caressed it, she submitted with apathy, and then her hand fell heavily on her knees; and my mother, dismayed, turned away to hide her grief.

Where was that vivacity now? where her activity and sprightliness, which kept up our spirits, and cheered us on during the first days of our adversity? From the moment she opened the door at Mesta, and appeared with her hair dishevelled, her breast uncovered, her dress torn and loosened, I never again saw that smile, nor heard that cheerful voice of hers. In that dark stable I heard nothing but her sobs, and now I looked upon her vacant stare and speechless lips. The happiness of her life was destroyed by the vile hands from which she tore herself away in order to save us. That dishonouring touch had withered the charm of her blooming youth. Her loveliness was still there, but without its former glow. She was beautiful still, but beautiful as the flower which a cruel hand has snatched from its stem, and has flung to the ground after crushing it.

Our ship glided swiftly on. Distance and the gathering darkness had gradually hid from our view the crests of Chio and Psara, and the outlines of the islands in the Ægean, towards which we shaped our course, could just be seen on the horizon like dim clouds.

Night soon came on; it was dark, no moon appeared; but the wind still blew fair, speeding us along over the foaming sea.

Fatigue and darkness, and the sense of security, the reaction of past emotions, the chill of night—all this gradually subdued and overcame the fugitives, who were crowded together on deck. Each tried to cover himself up as best he could; mothers hid their little ones in their bosoms; and old men laid their gray heads on the hard planks of the ship. The murmur of conversation was hushed, and nothing could be heard but the roar of the waves as they were ploughed up by the sharp bows of the ship, and the creaking of its timbers whenever the wind, freshening, weighed down upon the sails.

But I could not sleep. I sat up, leaning

my head against the mast, and gazing on the clouds and the stars as they appeared amidst them, while my mind was absorbed in thoughts of Adriana. I remembered the time of our childhood; I thought of her when she opened the door on our return from Smyrna, and of the joy which filled my heart when I saw her after the lapse of so many years. I recollected no end of incidents during our last hapless days at Chio, and her image was inseparable from these recollections. Her very voice, that cheerful ringing voice, seemed to re-echo in my ears.

The hours thus passed on, and gradually the stillness on board, the monotonous murmur of the waves, and the measured roll of the ship, began to tell on my wearied body. Although not yet quite asleep, my thoughts began to verge on the realm of dreams; but suddenly I was startled by the sound of a heavy splash in the sea, and by cries of terror.

"She has fallen into the sea! She has fallen overboard!"

I was on the quarter-deck in an instant. Adriana was not at her place. Some of the men were looking over the bulwarks into the sea, while the women cried out, "She has fallen into the sea. Save her! save her!"

The captain gave orders to clue up the sails; the ship's pace was slackened, and a boat was at once lowered. But the wind was now blowing hard, and we had left behind us that unknown spot where the sinister splash was first heard.

Oh, I never felt my hatred of the Turks more overpowering than at that moment.

I jumped into the boat before the captain had time to stop me. The sailors handled their oars with a will, and we retraced the ship's course. We kept silent in the hope of hearing her voice. We cried aloud, so as to be heard. There was no reply. We scanned the sea around us, and watched the rise of each wave. But not a sign of life. Presently a white speck on the surface of the water met my eye. I pointed it out to the sailors; they row again; we approach. It was Adriana's white head-dress!

We lingered long about that spot, but nothing could be seen, nothing could be heard, save the captain's orders to return to the ship. We went back. I held in my hand the white kerchief—the same one which, when on her return from Smyrna I saw her for the first time, I pulled loose and her hair fell on her shoulders. That kerchief was all that remained of her. I kept it then, and I have since treasured it as a sacred relic, as a cherished memorial.

VI.

When amidst the comforts of a London house I sit surrounded by my children, with so many dear relatives and prosperous countrymen near me,—when, in the enjoyment of the repose and well-being of to-day, I recollect the past, and I compare the calmness attending the close of my life with the sorrows, the dangers, and the privations of that eventful time,—I am myself amazed how we contrived to tide over and support such sufferings, how we ever emerged out of those cruel trials with our faculties unimpaired and bodies whole.

Often do the reminiscences of my youth seem to me as a dream, and the appalling devastation amid which I grew into manhood a myth. For those sufferings were common to us all; the struggle against fate was general, and for whole years together I passed my life seeing around me misery in all its developments.

Nor was our family the most unfortunate one in that general reign of adversity. On the contrary. True, we also had to fly; we had passed through many dangers, we had lost everything; but we at least were all safe together on a free soil, and poor Adriana's death alone had left a gap in our family circle.

But, both on board the ship which saved us from Chio, and now at Mykonos,—and at Tinios later, and again in every part of Greece, wherever our wandering steps took us,—we met everywhere with many others much more to be pitied than we.

So long as we remained at Chio, encircled by adversities, which tossed us to and fro, we knew not all the details of that indiscriminate martyrdom. Each one then thought of his own safety, and had no leisure to inquire into the condition of others, or to speak of his own woes. But when we rested our wearied heads, without the fear of a sword held ready over us, when we sat at the doorstep of a hospitable refuge which no Turk's shadow could darken, and each saw his own sorrow reflected in his neighbour's face, then we began to inquire into each other's sufferings, and search for absent relatives and friends.

How often did I not search in vain; how often, remembering our last meeting outside the chapel, did I not seek to trace the fate of those who were then of our little circle! But I could learn nothing. I thought especially of little Despina, of our last walk, of her bitter forebodings, and her silent tears, and I fancied I could still hear her sweet childish voice—"They will kill my father; they will kill him!"

It was then, however, I learnt of many a heartrending incident in that bloody period of the history of Chio—of many a fearful scene in that interminable tragedy. Each family had its own long tale of woe. Many had seen father, son, wife, slaughtered before their eyes. Many orphan children, saved and brought together, wailed their captive mothers; many mothers sought for their children in vain.

The cruel recollections of the past, the mourning for dear ones, murdered or carried into slavery, the bitterness of exile, the uncertainty of the future, the scarcity even of our daily bread, rendered that period of general disaster unbearable. Nevertheless, most of us went through it steadfastly; we struggled against adversity, and we emerged from the strife successfully.

When our young people, who have been born and bred in happier days, when they see us old men still robust and jovial, they perchance hesitate to credit the narrative of our early sufferings. And when, in a few years, the generation of our War for Independence shall have passed away, and the recital of our reminiscences by word of mouth shall have ceased, our grandchildren will not easily realise with what sacrifices and what tortures their well-being and our national regeneration have been purchased.

Therefore I should wish that more of the survivors of that time would write their memoirs. For out of the history of individuals that of nations is formed; and the history of Greek regeneration does not consist alone of the mighty deeds of our champions by sea and by land, but also of the persecutions, the massacres, the outrages on defenceless and weak creatures; their steadfastness amid misfortunes; their faith in God, which strengthened and ultimately realised, though it be partially, our hopes of a better future.

For all this let us bless the name of God; and may we, older men, die with the hope that our national aspirations will in the future be fulfilled in their integrity. But may the Almighty spare the younger generations of Greeks the trials we experienced. May our martyrdom be accepted by Fate as an ample expiation for all future time!

Whilst I write these lines, the reminiscences

of the past press thickly on my memory, and the incidents of those calamities pass in quick succession through my mind. I shut my eyes, and I see before me our wretched fellow-exiles; I hear their tales of woe; their sighs re-echo in my ears; I see them shed tears of bitterness, and wring their hands in despair.

Fifty years have passed away, and the earth has reclaimed most of them. Yet a goodly number still survive, sufficient to form a link between the past and the present. I could even name them. I could especially refer to that lady of high birth, now old, who, hiding then her beauty under the rags of a mendicant, traversed the depths of Asia Minor in quest of her child. God took pity upon her, and she returned with her child in her arms. And that other old lady, now the mother of honourable Greek citizens, who, when in the flower of her youth, was carried away into a Turkish harem, and after languishing there for two years, was ransomed with much difficulty at the very time her savage ravisher was expected to return from the war.

But is there a single one of my old compatriots who has no adventures to relate, often surpassing in dramatic incident anything the fertile imagination of the novelist can conceive? Only the other day one of them related in my presence how he, then ten years of age, served as a slave in the house of a Turk, and how, on the day when the hostages were hung, the Turk led him by the hand to the corner of the street, that he might witness the procession of those martyrs pass by. Amongst them was his father. He saw him, and tearing himself from the grasp of the Turk, he flew into his arms. His father snatched him up, pressed him to his bosom, gave him a kiss—one single kiss, and, putting him on the ground, thrust him afar from him, as if afraid lest the child should be carried along with him to the scaffold. The poor boy was afterwards ransomed, but that last embrace of his father's was never to be effaced from his memory. My old friend's eyes were dim with tears, and his voice faltered as he related to us this, his earliest recollection in life.

My object is not to speak of others. Yet how can I, while writing of my life, fail to remember that general disaster which surrounded us? We all suffered together; the ties of common trials, and the struggles for existence, mutually sustained us in fortitude, and gradually inspired us with courage.

During the first days we felt as if giddy, and no one thought of the morrow. The emotions consequent upon our flight and our escape were still recent, and the ready hospitality of the people of Mykonos, together with the little money which remained to us, sufficed for our maintenance. But our means were soon exhausted, and the islanders, being themselves poor, could certainly not maintain us. Misery was all-pervading, and there was but little money about. I remember, after we had spent our last ducat, my vain endeavours to sell a ring of my mother's. It was with much difficulty that I succeeded, later on, in finding a buyer at Spetzæ in the person of one of the most wealthy primates of that island. And even he bought it, as I feel convinced, simply in order to help us at a time of sorrow and distress. For those who had money then did not purchase jewels, either for use or as a speculation.

It now seems to me a miracle, how, in the midst of that general want, we contrived by degrees to find the means of livelihood and create commercial enterprise. Those who took refuge in Russia or Italy, or elsewhere, amid wealthy communities, had to struggle against no such difficulties in order to earn their bread in the sweat of their brow. But in Greece, what value could work possess at a time when all were poor and needy? And yet we managed to live, but how?

Two weeks ago I followed to his last rest one of my old friends. This wealthy merchant, who has left millions to his heirs, I remember him well selling sweetmeats in the still shapeless streets of Syra.

These sweetmeats were manufactured by his beautiful wife, the daughter of one of the principal families of Chio. And pray do not imagine that those who bought their wares were in a more enviable position.

But here again my pen is wandering, and leads me in advance of the order of my tale.

Two or three weeks after our arrival at Mykonos, we began, with my father, to think seriously what we should do, for somehow or other we had to work for the subsistence of our family. Our business was commerce; but commerce, in however humble a way, requires capital, failing which it cannot be improvised. Where was capital to come from? Some jewels, which my mother had saved, were of no avail. The things we had buried under the old apple-tree, being plate in silver and gold, might be converted into money more readily. But these we could not lay our hands upon. Our goods in the khan of Smyrna, and our uncollected credits, we did not even think of.

As to our property at Chio, heaven knew what Turk feasted upon it. We had absolutely nothing, and it was in vain my father unfolded and refolded the few documents he carried in his pocket-book.

Amongst these papers there was a letter from Venice, received the day previous to our departure from Smyrna. This letter reported the shipment of two cases of caps on board a British vessel, which was to have touched at several ports before arriving at Smyrna. My father, while at Chio, had sent the bill of lading to a friend of his at Smyrna, an Ionian, and consequently an English subject. But we had not received any answer, and my father thought no more of the caps. The letter from Venice, however, reminded me of the circumstance, and on these two cases I built up a magnificent structure of hopes and projects.

"You need not trouble yourself about it," said my father. "For if you expect to cover your head with those caps, you had better make up your mind to go bareheaded."

"Let us try," I replied. "There is no harm in writing."

I wrote, therefore, to our friend at Smyrna, and my father signed the letter, requesting that the caps should be sent to the care of the British consul at Mykonos. The worthy Mykoniote, who represented England, wearing a cap with a gold band round it, promised to forward the letter to Smyrna, and to make every endeavour to recover the two cases.

My father smiled incredulously, and, to say the truth, there was no great probability of our venture succeeding after the lapse of so long a time, in the midst of that general convulsion and the almost total interruption of communication, then difficult at best.

Anyhow, as we could certainly not procure means of subsistence by simply awaiting the result, we decided, as a last resource, to offer our services to the Provisional Government, not, of course, as soldiers, but as employés in some other civil capacity. For this purpose it was necessary to proceed to Nauplia, or rather Argos, which was then the seat of Government. But supposing we failed in this attempt also? Supposing our services were not accepted! We were sure to find ourselves in competition with others perhaps more capable, or backed by recommendations and patronage, of which we were completely devoid.

After turning these things over in our minds, and after obtaining friendly advice and information, we came to the conclusion that before starting for Argos we should arm ourselves with a letter of recommendation to Theodore Negris, who was Principal Secretary for Foreign Affairs, and President of the Council, and was considered as the pivot and life of the Executive. Such an introduction could be obtained through George Mavroyenis, an intimate friend of Negris, then residing at Tinos.

Many years previously, after the tragic death of the Grand Drogman Mavroyenis, this son of his took refuge at Chio with his sister. Both were still young, and, having taken up their abode near the house of my maternal grandfather, they frequented my mother's home, and became her bosom friends. They had since left Chio, but my mother had not forgotten them; and, judging by her own sentiments, she pressed me to repair to Tinos, and solicit, in her name, the protection of the friends of her childhood.

I hesitated and wavered. How present myself? They did not know my father's very name, and after the lapse of so many years, they might well have forgotten that of my mother's family also. But even in the event of their retaining some recollection of it, would they extend to me their acquaintance; would they receive me as the son of an old friend? Necessity, however, and my mother's urging, overcame my doubts, and, taking passage in a Myconiote caïque, I arrived one evening at Tinos.

When I landed on the little esplanade by the beach, it was already dark. I was at a loss where to seek shelter for the night, but on the esplanade I found the door of a coffee-house still open. There I obtained permission to rest till next morning, and I made myself snug on a wooden bench in a corner of the tavern, hoping to go to sleep. Such hope, however, was soon dispelled. The place was presently filled with Tiniotes, who were evidently in a festive mood, and the night was spent in music, singing, and drinking.

With what aching of heart I passed that night! I saw them from my dark corner, and heard them, but their joviality brought tears to my eyes, and the sound of their music reminded me of wailing and weeping. I ran over in my mind all our troubles since the revolution broke out, and I was astounded how these men had the heart to be merry.

My anger was no doubt unjust, and my pretensions unreasonable. Tinos could not be expected to look upon the state of affairs in the same light as Chio. Turks had not appeared on the island, nor was there any fear of their landing in order to massacre and enslave its inhabitants. The Tiniotes had remained unmolested, and, instead of hostile hordes, they saw around them a free Greece.

Besides, the Revolution was still in the flush of its first successes, which were even magnified by the lively Greek imagination. The utter collapse of the insurrectionary movement in Walachia had not yet become known, and while we at Chio fled in terror, at Tinos they believed Ypsilantis was marching southward in triumph, and that the Sultan's throne was tottering; the conviction was even general that in a very short time we might take possession of Constantinople, so that the Tiniotes might well consider themselves justified in making merry. The café, meanwhile, re-echoed with their patriotic songs, varied now and then by the mandoline's effusions in a more tender key.

Besides—for, in sum, the Tiniotes themselves did not lie on a bed of roses—man cannot weep for ever; his soul cannot endure unbroken grief. The necessity of pleasure and joy overpowers him at times, and while sorrow presses upon him, flashes of laughter break through the clouds of sadness. There are men who delight in grief and perpetuate mourning, but such dispositions are not natural. Nature possesses the power of healing wounds, and the heart of man tends in the end towards cheerfulness, and seeks after pleasure. For God, indeed, created man out of earth—heavy and humid earth—but He afterwards exposed this clay to the light of the sun, and man has retained the vivifying warmth of those rays.

That night, however, I did not so moralise. I had no experience of life as yet, and my sufferings were but recent. Later on, when most of us Chiote fugitives, coming together, began to put up hastily the first huts from which has since sprung the town of Syra, while war was still raging and want often oppressed us, this desire for mirth and pleasure took possession of us; and amidst that community of unhappy exiles, cheerfulness found its place. Never in the whole course of my existence do I remember a more lively period than those first years of our sojourn at Syra. True, I was still in the first glow of youth, but I can recollect that even the old men joined us in our merrymakings.

Towards early dawn quietness was at last restored in the café, and I fell asleep. When I got up I started at once for Mavroyenis' house, thinking, the while, what I should say, and how I should present myself. I had misgivings as to the reception in store for me, and I doubted the success of the step I had taken.

What was my surprise when, on the door being opened, and before I had time to utter a single word of the little speech I had prepared on my way, I heard a female voice cry out, "It is her son, her son!"

And she who had spoken these words came bounding down the steps. It was the daughter of our gardener. Having fled from Chio, she escaped to Tinos, and there entered the service of Mavroyenis. Neither he nor his sister had forgotten my mother. In fact, it was the mention of her name which had opened their hospitable door to the poor daughter of our old servant.

I asked her what had become of her father. The unfortunate girl could not say. They separated when a band of Turks had fallen upon the neighbourhood of our tower, and she fled with the other women. God only knew if her old father was dead or alive. Such were her pitiful replies, interrupted by sobs and tears.

I went up the steps with a lighter heart than when I knocked at the door. My host received me affably; he made me stay in his house, he gave me the desired letter of recommendation, and his encouraging words filled me with hope and comfort. As for his sister, she never ceased inquiring after my mother and the state of Chio, and the cruel sufferings of our flight. I was charmed with her sweetness, and impressed by her beauty and grace; but I hardly imagined, whilst admiring her, that she was destined to occupy a place in the history of our revolution, and that books would be written about her.

The remembrance of that kindly reception often restored my courage, and on many an occasion of difficulty in after life it strengthened my wavering confidence in the future. The recommendation did not ultimately prove of much avail, nor did Mavroyenis' patronage help me. But moral support, the expression of sympathy, a kindly word, a friendly smile, comfort the suffering mind more than any material aid.

By the help of God, such tokens of goodwill often refreshed me in the course of my protracted misery. So long as we prosper we have but few opportunities of appreciating the benevolence that is in our neighbours. It is only in days of adversity that we discover how man is naturally prone to charity and compassion, and how much he feels for those who suffer. After all, the wicked are few on this earth.

Next morning I returned to Mykonos, bearing the letter of introduction; and a few days later, meeting with a ship bound for the Gulf of Nauplia, we bade farewell to the hospitable little island, and our entire family sailed for the Morea.

VII.

THOSE who from childhood have been accustomed to traverse sea and land by steam have no conception of what travelling was in those days. It is only in our own Ægean Sea that even now, if we cannot wait for the fortnightly steamboat, we may yet find ourselves exposed to peregrinations not unlike those of Ulysses and his companions. But after all, the inhabitant of the very remotest of our islands is no longer the perpetual slave of the winds. If he be only patient enough, the steamer will call for him. In those days steamboats were unknown. Our skies had not yet smelt the smoke of coal, and our waves were still virgin to the flapping of paddle and screw.

The wind blew fair when we started from Mykonos; but it soon fell, and we found ourselves in a dead calm. For hours and hours together we saw immovable in front of us the rock of Syra, and the use of two ponderous oars did little to move our heavy lugger. At length the wind freshened again towards sunset, and the sails began to fill. But it blew from the south, and pushed us on to Andros. All night through we were on the tack, trying to get under shelter behind Cape Sunium, and after much trouble we succeeded next day in reaching the Piræus, there to take in fresh water.

When years later I again visited the port of Piræus, it appeared to me to have shrunk in size. Then it seemed enormous, for it was desolate. Our ship and two small fishing boats were the only craft floating on the expanse of its undisturbed waters. There, on the space now covered by its marble quays, the waves, slowly advancing, rolled on bare rock. Farther on, where a flourishing town now spreads out, and where large manufactories with their tall chimneys have sprung up, nothing was to be seen but a barren plain, the very picture of desolation. A solitary house by the beach, tottering into ruins, contributed to make the absence of animation and movement all the more apparent.

Athens was then besieged by the Greek troops, and a small detachment of armed men occupied that half-ruined house. But we did not hear any firing at that distance, nor did we see any other sign of hostilities, save that military occupation of the Piræus.

War is a savage business! It certainly does not tend to the improvement of human nature. Those soldiers we saw did us no harm; they placed no difficulties in our way. But I was glad when our ship moved off again. Their appearance had something harsh about it; their very greetings were terrifying.

On the third day of our departure from Mykonos we reached Spetzæ, the wind having prevented our sailing into the Gulf of Nauplia. The captain landed, and, wearied with the confinement on board ship, we followed his example, and had the satisfaction of again setting foot on dry land.

We sat on the rocks by the outskirts of the town, and we all kept silent, my father appearing very downcast. I had never seen him look so depressed. He seemed ailing, but he did not complain. He only held his head between his hands, and his eyes were heavy and dim.

We were alone there, but farther on we could see the bustle and movement of the townsfolk on the beach. The harbour was full of shipping, and our boat lay moored on the rocks, awaiting the return of the captain.

My eyes were fixed on the little craft. I was thinking what would become of us if my father were taken ill; and I remembered our tower and his comfortable quarters in it, when I saw a young Spetziote approach.

"Welcome, Christian brethren," said he. "Do you come from Chio?"

"From Chio!" replied my father, lifting up his head with an effort.

"And why sit out here? why do you not come into the town?"

"We are going to Argos."

"To Argos! Argos is not the place for women and children. You had better stop here."

My father explained that we were going there in the hope of finding some means of livelihood. But the Spetziote went on to say that Argos was but a camp, and Nauplia was still besieged. He represented to us the inconvenience of the presence of women in the midst of such warlike scenes, and urged us to put off our departure.

While he was still speaking the captain returned, and corroborating the words of the young Spetziote, he recommended us to remain at Spetzæ.

There was no difficulty in prevailing upon us to remain. But where could we put up? Where lay our heads in this new station of our exile? The good Spetziote understood, apparently, the cause of our hesitation.

"Come to my house," he said. "My father was killed fighting; my mother died soon after him; and my house is now deserted. Stay in it as long as you please. Come."

We accepted with emotion the offer of that good and generous man. From that moment he became the staunchest of friends for me. We have since been like brothers to one another, and our friendship remained undisturbed to the hour of his death, a few years ago. He died full of honours, having proved himself a most worthy and upright servant of his country, both in war and in time of peace.

We now moved to the house of our new friend, and took possession of its spacious and comfortable rooms. My father soon began to feel his strength fail him. Perhaps he foresaw his end approach, and he did not wish to die without securing to his widow and his orphans their daily bread. He did not give expression to such forebodings; but that same day he urged me to proceed to Argos without delay, and making use of the letter of recommendation, solicit from Negris some employment.

Two days later I landed at the Mills of Nauplia, and thence I proceeded on foot to Argos.

Our Spetziote friend and the captain were perfectly right. Their words and my first impressions at the Piræus had already prepared me for what I was about to witness; but at the Piræus I had seen only in miniature what I now beheld. I found myself in a world quite new to me. The thousands of warriors in fustanellas, their haughty demeanour, their rude expressions, the contemptuous looks with which they measured every inch of me, their abrupt replies to my timid inquiries, the noise and the movement, and the confusion of the camp, all this troubled me. Certainly this was no place for women and children. I myself felt that I was not in a congenial atmosphere; I was not in my element.

When at last, Mavroyenis' letter in hand,

I succeeded in penetrating into the minister's presence, and saw before me, standing in front of a high desk, an ugly little man, I was taken aback, and I hesitated to believe that this was the principal Secretary of State, the great and renowned Theodore Negris. He was busy writing, and while waiting with the letter in my hand, I examined the scene around me. The little room was full of books—books on the table, books on the chairs, books on the strong box, books everywhere; and in their midst rose the high desk, and Negris stood by it writing. He was even shorter than I. I am convinced no feeling of self-love misled me into this estimate.

I looked at him, and I thought to myself, now, there he is; a puny, ugly, defenceless-looking man; and yet they all obey him— those savage warriors, and he governs them. Why? Because he is their superior in intellect and education. Intellect cannot be called into existence; but one may become learned. Good sense is the gift of God;

but knowledge may be acquired. Thus I reasoned then, forgetting that human intelligence is of many degrees and of various tendencies; that the power of regulating one's own will according to circumstances has not been given to all; nor yet the ability of imposing that will on one's fellow creatures. I overlooked such considerations; but while I gazed upon Negris I formed the resolution to add to my stock of knowledge; and, in fact, ever after that time I applied myself to reading and studying. Naturally I have not been able to do much. But whatever I learnt in after life, whatever thirst for knowledge there is in me, it dates from that hour—when I waited till Negris had done writing. That was the starting-point of my intellectual regeneration, though its extent may have remained necessarily restricted.

Negris at length laid down his pen, and asked me what I wanted. I silently held out my hand and presented to him the letter. Having read it, he bade me sit on the only vacant chair near him, and began questioning me what I knew, and what he could do for me. I felt I blushed as I attempted to enumerate my accomplishments, and to express the desire to obtain a clerkship under him.

"Very well," said he, when I had done; "very well. I have need of young men such as you, and I shall give you a suitable post. But we must first settle down a little. Wait until we take Nauplia, and then look in again."

Wait till Nauplia is taken! I left utterly dispirited. Why, for the last three weeks they had considered the capitulation of the fortress as certain, and the plenipotentiaries of the besiegers were already inside Nauplia negotiating the terms, while armed men gathered from every part of the surrounding country, in the hope of celebrating, each in his own fashion, this fresh triumph of the Greek arms. Yet the Turks had not surrendered, and Dram-Ali was on his way from Northern Greece at the head of a powerful army. The rumour of his progress southward spread, and had already begun to shake the confidence of many on our side. Such, at least, were the news I heard during my two days' sojourn at Argos. The tide of events seemed to be turning against us; and being still swayed by my impressions of Chio, I became a ready victim to fear. How was I to foresee then or hope that Colocotronis would annihilate Dram-Ali at Dervenaki?

On the second night, while tossing sleeplessly over the hard boards which served as a bed, I made up my mind as to what I should do. I was not destined for the life of camps. Commerce was my vocation.

Next morning I repaired to the Mills, where I was lucky enough to find a ship ready to start for Spetzæ, and I took my passage accordingly.

I have never since visited Nauplia, but the stern rock of Fort Palamidi remains imprinted on my mind, as it overshadowed the valley, where thickets of reeds fence in the course of a little stream, with the town spreading below, on the walls of which I could see from afar the crescent wave.

At Spetzæ I found both my parents and my sisters laid up with sickness. How much we then again felt the absence of poor Adriana! How often we all thought of her! It was I who had now to undertake, of necessity, the care of all the family. I became at one and the same time chambermaid, sick-nurse, and cook. The good housewives of our neighbourhood were amazed to see a man—contrary to all the usages of the island—stoop to such feminine work, and their thoughts were betrayed by the contemptuous smiles with which they accompanied their obliging offers of assistance.

Fortunately, the illness of my mother and sisters was but the temporary result of moral and physical prostration, and in a few days they one after the other left their beds. But my father was not destined to recover. I cannot say what was his illness. The so-called doctor whom we had recourse to, as soon as we began to be seriously alarmed, declared he was suffering from heart disease, and promised to cure him.

But evidently he did not know what he was about, and I doubt if he had ever set foot in a medical school of any kind. He was an old Maltese, who for many years past had exercised, not for humanity's sake alone, the calling of itinerant physician in many a Levantine city. At that time any Frank easily passed muster as a "doctor," and God only knows in what circumstances his Excellency was improvised into a physician. But gradually he must have persuaded himself that he was proficient in the science, while beneficent nature aided his efforts sometimes, and at others he himself conscientiously hurried on the end of his unfortunate patients.

Still my father remained prostrate. Fever undermined his already exhausted system, and agonising pains deprived him of rest. He felt death approach, and he awaited his end bravely. And we, forgetting our manifold privations of the time being, and our past comforts, thought only how to relieve his sufferings and how to save him, if possible. But our hopes disappeared day by day, as the cold hand of decay seemed to spread over his body.

One night I remained alone by his pillow, having with much difficulty prevailed upon my mother to take some rest in the adjoining room. My father had sunk into a torpor, which seemed like sleep. I sat near him, with my hands crossed, and while watching him my mind strayed away into sad thoughts. The sick-room was lit up only by the candle burning before the sacred icons, and the night was perfectly still. Suddenly I fancied I heard an unusual noise outside, and talking in the street. I crept to the window, and half opening the shutter, I distinguished the moving shadows of men. I dare not throw open the window for fear of awaking my father, who seemed reposing. But I tried to listen to what they were saying. I did hear, but I could not understand, for they spoke in Albanian. The word *Armàta*, however, which was often repeated, aroused my suspicions. Presently the doors were shut, and the shadows disappeared, bearing, as they seemed to me, cases and sacks on their shoulders. Silence again reigned supreme, but the word *Armàta* resounded in my ears. I knew enough to understand it meant a fleet. But to which fleet did they refer? I waited impatiently for the day, not knowing what to think of it all, and dreading fresh complications. I was involuntarily reminded of that first night at Smyrna, when the war-cries of the Turks had wakened me.

Towards dawn my mother returned to her post by the bedside of our patient, and sent me to rest. But instead of going to sleep, I quickly left the house. We were its only occupants, for our kind-hearted host lived on board his ship. From the extremity of the town, where our house lay, I descended towards the port, and, as I approached, I met with increasing animation and movement. I inquired what it all was about, and I was informed that on the island of Hydra they had lit up beacon-fires at nightfall.

"And what do the beacons signify?" I asked.

"That a Turkish fleet is descending toward us."

The Spetziotes had already transported on board their ships all their valuables, and were making ready, in case the Turks did in fact approach, to embark their women and children. They knew the enemy's fleet was powerful and numerous, and they were anxious about their homes, but they had every confidence in their floating fortresses.

In the port I met some of my compatriots who had taken refuge at Spetzæ. They also were making ready for escape. A vessel from Mytilene, under Russian flag, was anchored on the other side of the island, and they had sent to negotiate for a passage to Ancona. They offered to take us with them. But how could we leave? How move my father, who was on the point of death? And yet, how remain on the island if the Turks came to land?

I returned home in trouble and dismay. I beckoned to my mother to come out. I explained to her briefly how matters stood, and I asked her if she thought we might move my father. She led me by the hand to his bedside, and pointed towards him. He was still unconscious, his eyes were shut, his mouth half open, and he breathed heavily. Then for the first time I saw before me the agony of death, and the dying man was my beloved father.

My mother held my hand tight, and did not say a word in her efforts to subdue her anguish. Thus we stood by the bed, speechless and motionless, listening to the last agony of the dying man. I bent my head and kissed my mother's hand; she did not stoop to embrace me, but she only put her other hand on my head, and told me in a subdued voice, "Go, fetch a priest." I rushed out at once. I did not wish to give vent to my grief in her presence. At the door-steps I met the doctor, who was coming in.

"We have escaped it, my friend!" he cried cheerfully as soon as he saw me. But his expression was at once changed on seeing the trouble I was in, and lowering his voice, he inquired, "How is he getting on upstairs?"

I did not reply, but shook my head.

"I suppose it is all his fright at the Turks. But they have beaten a retreat, and we are safe."

I left him going up the steps, and I went my way with a lighter heart. At least, I thought to myself, he will die in peace, and the Turks will allow us to mourn him undisturbed.

The doctor's words brought back to my mind the horrors of Turkish invasion, and all the consequences which would have resulted from their presence on the island; and while I hurried on, I prayed God it might be true indeed that we were spared from the terrors of their appearance.

When I returned with the priest my father

still breathed heavily. Once only did he open his eyes, and his look betokened recognition of us; but he could not utter a word, and he again shut his eyes. His respiration grew more difficult, and he seemed to suffer for want of breath. The doctor lifted him on the bed, and my mother propped him up with pillows, while I cut his shirt open with a pair of scissors, that we might give some relief to his wearied lungs.

What was the sentiment which then moved my father in his last agony? Why did he frown and move his hand, as if wishing to prevent his shirt being torn? That incident remained indelibly impressed on my mind, and I revert to it involuntarily whenever I think of the vanity of the things of this world. Such is man! Death had already spread its black wings, and the last hour, eternal rest, darkness itself, was approaching. Yet the dying man, that good, loving old man, instinctively waved his hand, that he might save the bit of linen which covered his bosom!

His death-agony continued all day. Meanwhile the Turkish fleet moved away to the south. The danger passed away from over Spetzæ, and the islanders were again quiet.

Towards nightfall my father breathed his last. Next day I sold my mother's ring, and we buried our beloved dead in a humble and tombless grave.

It was the 5th of July 1822. Such dates are never forgotten.

VIII.

I was now left the head of the family, and its only support. It was I who must maintain it, I establish my sisters in life, I comfort my mother's old age. And for all resource I had but the promise given me by Negris to name me to a post when and after Nauplia had fallen. But something whispered within me that my prospects in life did not lie in that direction. My family traditions and my whole training had made a merchant of me; and I felt that commerce was my vocation. By it alone I could prosper and become useful to myself, to my family, to my country.

But how make a start? That was my difficulty. After paying for my father's burial I had left to me a little money out of the proceeds of the sale of the ring. It was an insignificant sum, hardly sufficient for our departure from Spetzæ—a plan I immediately began to consider.

Spetzæ was not the place for me. Business requires an orderly state of things, security and quietness. But how could these elements of social prosperity prevail on that heroic island while her citizens, sacrificing both their lives and their property in the unequal struggle against the foe, necessarily contracted the habit of despising life, and of setting violence and might before right and justice? Such were the natural consequences of those times. Without a pre-existing social organisation, without a strong Government, without regular resources, or any paramount centre, the insurrection nevertheless spread and prospered, thanks only to individual efforts and sacrifices. And in the midst of those convulsions, force was supreme, and the sword imposed individual will. The struggle was desperate. Its watchword—"Liberty or Death"—was no idle boast, no pompous phrase. For it was well known in advance how the Turks would act if resistance were once overcome. The fate of Chio was a terrible warning to Spetzæ and the other naval islands. Men, therefore, were led on by despair in that struggle, and the whole atmosphere breathed, so to say, savage cruelty.

Such a condition of things was not favourable to commerce. Who troubled himself then with police and courts of law? In presence of so much bloodshed, the very value of life had fallen in common estimation. One day a Ragusene trader was killed in the market-place, on account of a squabble with his customers over the choice of the sardines he sold. That incident effaced any hesitation I may still have had as to the advisability of our leaving Spetzæ, and I made up my mind definitely that we would return to Tinos. There the inhabitants were less warlike, milder in their habits, life generally was easier, and, thanks to Mavroyenis and the many refugees from Chio, I should consider myself less of a stranger at Tinos than elsewhere.

We therefore took leave of our good host with much aching at heart, and we quitted the island of Spetzæ and my father's grave there.

At Tinos I hired a small and modest house. I bought some bedding—the only furniture which our reduced balance of cash permitted us to indulge in—and I left the rest to Providence.

They are terrible things, poverty and want, coming after a comfortable existence. Still more cruel is the uncertainty about the bread of the morrow, when one has to look after an aged mother and sisters of tender years. And yet man gradually gets accustomed to everything.

When I was still bargaining with the landlord of the house, I remarked that he wore a new cap, but I paid no further attention to the matter. Next day, however, I met a Tinian who had evidently treated himself likewise to a new cap; a few steps farther I made the same remark, and then I saw another in a similar turn-out, and a fourth later on. Their caps were all of one colour and of the same shape; this coincidence moved my curiosity, and it immediately brought back to my mind the two cases sent to us from Venice. Without loss of time I hunted up our landlord.

"Just tell me," I said, "where did you buy that cap?"

"I bought it of the English Consul, but you won't find any more; he has sold them all off."

So it was the English Consul who sold the caps! That same day I was off to Mykonos, where I met my friend the Vice-consul. He was delighted to see me, and informed me that our two cases had been forwarded from Smyrna to Tinos, and that he had entrusted to his colleague there the disposal of their contents. He gave me a letter requesting him to recognise me as the proprietor of the goods.

I was now impatient to return; but my kind friend insisted I should accept his hospitality that night. Next day I took leave of him with expressions of sincere gratitude, and I returned to Tinos. Fortunately the winds favoured those peregrinations of mine.

On landing at Tinos, I made straight for the British Consulate. I cannot recollect the name of the good old Tiniote who at that time represented there the might and power of England; but I remember his clean-shaven face and his gold spectacles. He showed me the account of the sale of the caps, and he handed to me on the spot the net proceeds, amounting to five thousand piastres.*

Five thousand piastres! That wretched little sum appeared to me wealth inexhaustible. I cared neither to check the account, nor see how far it might have been possible to do better with the sale of the goods. The sum handed to me was an unexpected resource, which opened up to me the career of commerce. I was now a capitalist, in possession of five thousand piastres! I rushed to my mother to impart to her the news of

* About forty pounds sterling.

our good fortune; I showed her my treasure, I asked for her blessing, and, full of hopes and projects, I sailed for Syra two days later.

Large ships did not touch at Tinos for want of a harbour; but they went on to Syra, which port was considered even by the Turks as neutral. The Catholic inhabitants of that island had taken no part in the insurrection, and did not even recognise its existence. On the summit of the cone-like hill, on which the town was built, the white flag of France represented the protection they had sought and obtained. The whole population of the island was confined to those who lived on that steep and barren hillside. Over the extent of ground now covered by the wealthy city of Hermoupolis, one could then see bare rocks only. On the very spot where the band now enlivens the marble-flagged esplanade, and where the ladies of Syra trail their long silk gowns, some small cabbage gardens and a few fruit trees betokened the industrious habits of the poor islanders. The only buildings near the sea were three or four wine-stores and a small catholic chapel. Next to these, they had lately put up on the beach a miserable little café, which served also as a hotel, as a counting-house, and as an exchange. Farther on, where the shipbuilding yards now extend, and where the measured ring of the hammer enlivens the scene, the carcass of a shipwrecked merchantman covered the desolate shore. Such was Syra when for the first time I and two or three other Chiotes—the pioneers of the future commercial development of that island—had taken up our abode in the solitary café, awaiting the arrival of some vessel, on the chance of doing business in its cargo.

It was not long before a ship arrived from Russia. That was the first transaction in which I had to take the initiative, and which I was to carry through alone, being no longer guided by the advice and experience of my poor father. I trembled lest I should risk my capital in some bad venture. I visited the goods on board the ships a third and a fourth time, I considered the matter negotiated, made my calculations, and recast my estimates; I hesitated long; at last I made up my mind. I bought salt-fish for the sum of one thousand piastres; I shipped them on board a Tiniote smack, I took passage in her myself, I made the sign of the cross, and we sailed.

At Tinos, the rule had been established that all eatables should first be exposed for sale in the market-place during three days, so that the people might provision themselves; and at the expiration of that time the retail traders might treat for the remainder. I was naturally obliged to conform to the prevailing usage; but I was not at all disposed to place myself behind my barrels, and to retail publicly my fish, one at a time. Notwithstanding all my mishaps, I had not forgotten our old dignified habits. I therefore tried at first to find some one who could conveniently replace me; but the ill-success of my first inquiries, and above all, the example set by the other traders, decided me to put aside my dignity, and to undertake personally the sale of my goods.

Here I was, then, retailer of salt-fish in open market. I took up a suitable post on the small esplanade by the jetty, and I began with some timidity at first to invite customers. It was still very early, yet buyers were not wanting; my fish found favour, and business went on briskly. As the sale progressed, I got accustomed to the work: the fervour of success took possession of me, and urged on my zeal; and, emulating the example of those near me, I praised my goods and raised my voice, so as to draw customers. Thus I soon overcame the first timidity of gesture and awkwardness.

While I was still in the heat of the business, I heard a noise somewhere in front of me, and, looking up, I saw in the house opposite a fair-haired maiden open the window and fix the shutters, which were being battered by the wind against the wall. This done, she folded her arms on the ledge, and, leaning forward, turned her face towards me. Her looks troubled me, and my commercial ardour was paralysed. How could I cry out and call for custom when the eyes of so fair a girl were on me? I tried to go on with my work; but my thoughts were in the window, and there my looks were often directed. Presently I see her smile. Why that smile? Is she making fun of me; or is it a sign of recognition? I felt agitated; a blush came over my cheeks; and no longer paying due attention to what I was about, I gave to a buyer double the quantity of fish he had paid for. I soon discovered my mistake, and turned round to call him back, when, at the doorstep of the house behind me, I saw a young Tiniote leaning with his shoulder against the wall, his arm bent on his waist, and his head turned towards the window opposite. His amorous glances were a revelation to me. The rays which beamed from the eyes of the fair maiden passed clean over my head; they were not meant for me, nor could I have any claim to her smiles.

The lesson was not lost upon me. I resumed my work with my former ardour, and went on selling.

In two days I had disposed of my stock of fish with a profit of twenty per cent, and I was again off to Syra. I returned with a consignment of olive oil, which I got rid of, realising a profit of eight per cent. I next invested in caviar with equal success; and so I continued my operations very briskly. Profits grew more moderate as competition increased; but my labours continued to be well recompensed, and in a few months, after maintaining our family, and restoring a certain amount of comfort within our humble home, my capital had already grown from five to eight thousand piastres.

Since that time I have realised many profits, and I have sustained many a loss. Thanks to God, the credit side of my books has always been in advance of the debit, so that I have now the satisfaction to know that my labours have assured a comfortable existence to my children. But the sweetness of those first profits, insignificant though they were, I have never since experienced; nor has any satisfaction resulting from subsequent commercial ventures ever equalled my joy over the net balance left by the sale of the salt-fish. The production of something from almost nothing, the success of my own first combinations in trade, the conviction that I was in a position not to allow my mother and sisters to starve, the hope which such a beginning gave me for the future—all this increased manifold the value and the enjoyment of those first profits.

I do not pretend to say that afterwards I carried on my operations in a kind of philosophic indifference. No; my zeal did not diminish subsequently; for success is always gratifying. But my enthusiasm was moderated, and the pleasure of gain was gradually blunted. Having once made certain that I had secured to myself material independence, and that I possessed the means to render my family's existence a comfortable one, the palpitations of delight with which I closed my balance-sheets ceased. For the accumulation of riches is not in itself a source of happiness. Independence, that is what should be the true and healthy mainspring of the exertions of a hard-working man.

I was not then the only young Chiot who was striving how to produce a unit out of nothing, and how to convert two into four. There were many others, with whom common misfortune and daily intercourse in the market-place of Tinos, or the desolate beach of Syra, had brought me into contact. Amongst these was the betrothed of my eldest sister, who had also taken refuge at Tinos, after an odyssey of sufferings. The affianced of my younger sister was made a slave by the Turks, and no one had since heard what had become of him. I also was betrothed from childhood, but I became a widower before marriage, my promised wife having died years ago. And the whirlwind of the revolution broke upon us before my father had time to arrange a fresh match for me.

Such were the customs of Chio. Each family was anxious to form alliances with its equals, and as choice was restricted, the competition for suitable parties began at an early age. The aristocratic exclusiveness of those who intermarried, and the narrow limits of Chiot society, necessarily brought about in the end marriages between near relatives.

I have no desire to commend that practice of our fathers—the early betrothals, whereby they themselves sealed the most important contract in life, without the knowledge or consent of the interested parties. Still they might plead in their justification the success of such matches. The young people were brought up from childhood, the one, so to say, for the other; and conjugal attachment was preceded by a long acquaintance, and the habit of mutual devotion. Marriage, coming after this period of a long betrothal, had none of the heart-beating, none of that reciprocal unacquaintance as to the past, none of that uncertainty of the future, which accompanies love matches as a rule. Life was prepared for, and passed without violent emotions; nor did this diminish the quiet happiness of families.

But under the altered circumstances of our present national life this old custom would only degenerate, as it has done, into the consideration of material interests alone, and into questions of dowry, so that I shall not be sorry to see it abolished.

Besides, everything has changed with us since that time. Then younger men were guided by those advanced in years; and this they considered but natural, and a thing not admitting of discussion. Under that discipline, and living in such close union, families became strong, and their power was increased by the ties of those intermarriages. Herein lies one of the explanations of the success of Chiotes, not only in the management of their municipal affairs before the revolution, but also of their commercial organisation after the destruction of Chio.

Howbeit, at that time we had not yet

changed our ways, but remained under the influence of our traditions and of our training. So that I considered the betrothed of my eldest sister as a brother already, and I was anxious to betroth the younger one as soon as possible. Nor was I long in fixing upon one of my friends, whom those hard times did not prevent from facing the responsibilities of a married life. I submitted my choice to my mother's approval, and thus we betrothed the younger sister also.

With my two future brothers-in-law we decided to enter into partnership, each contributing one thousand piastres to the common fund, the conditions being, that one of us should remain at Tinos and sell, the other go to Syra for purchases, and the third accompany the goods shipped from Syra to Tinos. The lot fell upon me to serve as buyer, and, provided with the best part of our capital, I took leave of my mother, and embarked on board a lugger ready to sail for Syra. But we were still hauling in the anchor when I saw a boat making for us in all haste, and in her my two partners, motioning with their hands, to stay our departure. Coming alongside, they brought us the disagreeable news that the plague had broken out on board a ship which had come from Constantinople to Panormos, one of the small bays of Tinos, and that information of this event had already been transmitted from Panormos to Syra, so that it was certain they would not receive us there for fear of the epidemic, nor could they permit communication with Tinos to continue. It was consequently resolved that I should disembark, and put off my departure till the fears of epidemic were allayed. Unfortunately, the plague was communicated from the ship to the islanders, and although it was neither serious nor very deadly, yet it was sufficient to frighten all the surrounding islands, and to shut us up at Tinos.

Thus our plans were frustrated, our association was wrecked, and I remained without occupation. My enforced inactivity was the more tedious, coming after the movement and animation of the last few months.

In other respects, we lived very quietly at Tinos, nor did the fear of the Turk and the tumult of war disturb our thoughts as formerly.

One day, however, in the beginning of October, it seemed as if the turn of Tinos had come at last, and that the black wings of calamity were again overshadowing us. But now I breathed in a more manly atmosphere, and my spirit was upheld by the example of those around me. Therefore, instead of thinking of flight, I also prepared to resist and to fight.

The sea between Syra and Mykonos was covered wrth Turkish ships, there becalmed for many hours. We saw the boats of one of them make for the shores of Mykonos. Firing ensued, and amidst the smoke we could make out the boats returning to the ship. These movements appeared like the preliminaries of a projected landing, and of an attack by the fleet. The church bells at

Tinos were therefore set ringing, the islanders ran to arms, and even I lent a hand in moving an old gun, and placing it in position on a prominent hill—Cape Pacha, as it was called.

But we had no cannon balls, and confined ourselves to burning powder, by way of menacing and braving the Turks. And standing on that hill, and busying myself to no purpose, I listened to that vain firing, and looked upon the Turkish ships, thinking all the while of our past misfortunes during the flight from Chio, and anxiously awaited the result.

Luckily the fortitude of the men of Tinos was not put to a more severe test. The Pacha took no notice of us, nor did he attempt to punish the Mykoniotes, although they had killed some of his men during the repulse of his boats. Taking advantage of the freshening wind, he soon disappeared from amidst our islands.

From that day we were no more disturbed. Indeed we might almost have forgotten that we were within the sphere of the struggle, but for the constant resounding of its stirring events. When, above all, we heard of the burning of the Turkish flag-ship, and the defeat of the enemy's fleet at Chio, an indescribable enthusiasm took possession of all us refugees, who saw in the mighty deed of Kanaris a revenge for the destruction of our island. Dram-Ali's annihilation at Dervenaki, the raising of the first siege of Messolonghi, and the other successive triumphs of the first years of the insurrection, raised our hopes and strengthened our confidence.

Psara and Cassos had not yet been destroyed; Mehement Ali's intervention, through the invasion of Crete, had not yet commenced; heroic Messolonghi had not yet fallen, nor had the intestine dissensions and the sacrilegious civil strife yet begun. Every movement prospered, and the hand of God seemed to help the arms of Greece; so that seeing the insurrection thus take root and thrive, we looked forward to a prompt and happy issue.

The third year of the war now commenced, while the almond-trees of Tinos were being clothed in their spring blossoms. Impatient with long inactivity, and living on thoughts and projects, I conceived the idea of proceeding to Chio and trying to recover the treasure we had buried in our garden. I called to mind my father's words when we had done covering over the sacks in the trench under the apple-tree. He had departed this life; and I remained the protector and support of the family, and the recovery of that reserve fund might facilitate now both my sisters' marriage, and perhaps my journey to Europe also.

The more I turned the matter over in my mind the more the desire to realise it took root, and the elaboration of my project occupied me constantly. I thought of it alone, and, asleep or awake, I dreamt of its execution.

Some of my compatriots had already gone to Chio secretly, and had returned safe and sound. The authorities there had orders from Constantinople to favour the return of

Christians, and not to disturb them. Such was my information, and the experience of those who had returned encouraged me. I therefore communicated my intentions to my mother, who, fearing the worst, tried by every means to dissuade me. But my resolve was unshaken. I saw all its dangers clearly, and I owned that the enterprise was a reckless one. But an irrepressible impulse spurred me on to its execution, and I paid no heed to my mother's remonstrances. I delivered to her keeping my small fortune, begged for her blessing, and I left disguised as a peasant.

The caique on which I took passage had a cargo of wheat to dispose of in some of the more outlying ports of Chio, and the master, Captain Kephala, promised to land me on some safe spot. When he saw me appear on board in my large white trousers and my peasant's vest, and armed with two little kegs of red caviar, he laughed heartily. I joined in the laughter, but I confess I then began to think more of my mother than of the treasure under the apple-tree.

IX.

THE wind blew from the south, and our caique bounded on, making good way towards Chio. But as night advanced the rapidity of its movements, under a freshening wind, increased to a disagreeable degree. Those who know the Ægean must have experienced how troublesome the southerly wind can become there. Then for the first time I was overpowered by sea-sickness. Lying stretched on the after-deck, I felt the ship rise and fall under me, and I heard the noise of the sea angrily beating against its sides, while the waves simmered into foam, the wind whistled through the rigging, and the rudder creaked, labouring within its socket.

I kept my eyes shut, but I remained sleepless all night. My body felt heavy, and I possessed neither the will nor the power to move. I was often drenched by the waves, but I could neither stir from my place nor call for help.

About midnight I heard Captain Kephala tell the man at the rudder that if the wind increased he would make jetsam of a part of the cargo. Jetsam! and then what would become of my two kegs? For they lay on the top of the wheat, and would be the first to be sacrificed. It was with those two barrels I purposed traversing Chio as an itinerant vendor of caviar until I reached our tower. Without them my plans were frustrated and my hopes disappeared. I wished to speak to the captain, and beg of him to spare my barrels, or at least not throw them both overboard. But I could neither move nor utter a word.

The caique meanwhile rose and bumped violently back upon the waves, and I now began to fear lest danger menaced not the barrels alone. But our caique was a solid and smart little boat, and few seamen knew their business better than Captain Kephala. Next morning found us anchored in a safe and quiet little creek on the southern coast of Chio.

The land around the creek was cultivated, but there were no houses; only on the rising ground, at a considerable distance from the sea, amidst well-wooded hills, the rays of the sun were reflected on the white-washed cottages of three or four little villages. Nearer the beach another caique was moored, and we could see some peasants with their beasts of burthen stand near by the shore.

It is a sweet and potent feeling, the love of one's country! When from on board the caique I looked upon the scene before me— the blooming nature, the distant villages, and the little knot of people on the sands— my heart leapt with joy. I saw Chio once more; and those peasants were my compatriots! The little caique by the beach lent life to the scene, and I gazed upon it with inward satisfaction, thinking that all was not ruin and desolation on our island.

But soon there was a revulsion in these thoughts, and I wished the little craft had never been there. It had come from Psara, also with a cargo of wheat for sale, and the simultaneous arrival of our caique brought about a deplorable conflict. The men from Psara were by no means disposed to submit to peaceful competition; but, by means of threats, wished to compel our captain to quit that improvised market, on which they declared they had secured the rights of priority. Kephala, on the other hand, would not yield, but insisted, upholding the principles of free trade. From words the controversy threatened to result in acts of violence; fists were shaken, and knives leapt from their sheaths. But I know not how it all ended; for, while the dispute was raging, I landed stealthily with my two kegs, and having arranged with one of the peasants to carry them on his ass, we started on our way towards the village.

My guide, a young peasant of twenty, robust, good-natured, and sprightly, soon gained my confidence. Before reaching our journey's end I had already obtained full details of his humble existence; and I, on my part, revealed to him my name and descent, but not the principal object of my return to Chio. I conjured him not to make known to any one that I was a Chiot of the town. He promised, and kept his word faithfully; during the whole time of my sojourn on the island he protected me, and behaved to me as a true friend. His is one more name I must add to the list of those brave and generous souls whose comforting sympathy helped me on during my journey through this long vale of tears.

When we approached the village the good Pandéli deposited my barrels in a ruined wine-press in the corner of a vineyard by the wayside, and bade me wait for him there till he first went on with his ass to the village, and made sure there were no Turks in it. I sat at the root of an olive-tree under the shadow of the wall, and I waited, my eyes fixed on the turn of the road whence I expected soon to see Pandéli reappear. There was complete silence around me, the grasshoppers alone, exulting under the rays of the sun, disturbing the stillness of the air.

Suddenly the laughter of children resounded near me. On turning round I saw four little urchins, their inquisitive eyes fixed upon me, but as soon as our glances met they hid behind the wine-press. In a few minutes a fresh band of boys appeared, with their fingers in their mouths. They looked at me for an instant with an air of amazement, and then, turning tail, they ran away. Others came after them, and I began to feel anxious about this inquisitorial ordeal at the hands of the young generation of the village. My uneasiness was turned into impatience as Pandéli's absence was prolonged, and his tardiness excited my suspicions. At length I saw him approach, but, in place of his ass, another peasant accompanied him.

"There are no Turks," said he. "Come along with us, Loutzi."

Without further explanations they each

lifted one of the kegs on their shoulders, and we all three entered the village. In the little central market-place we found gathered in a knot a number of peasants, who surrounded my two guides, and a discussion ensued amongst them in an undertone. Presently, however, it assumed the importance of a lively controversy, which compelled Pandéli and his friend to lay the kegs on the ground, so as to allow free play to their gesticulations, and full scope to their tongues. The rapidity with which they all spoke together was such that their confused hubbub did not enable me to make out what they were saying, though I concluded that I was the object of their discussions. Finally an understanding or a compromise was apparently arrived at; and, again taking up the kegs, my two protectors made way through the crowd on the village green, and we proceeded to Pandéli's house.

"Will you not tell me what it is all about?" I asked him, as soon as we had got clear of the crowd.

"It is nothing, Loutzi; we will make it all right."

His reply was laconic; but there was something reassuring in his tone, as well as in the manner in which he pronounced my name, with the peculiar phonetic modulation of the K. I did not ask for more explanations; but everything made it clear to me that the fear of the Turk still hovered in the air of Chio.

Pandéli had been recently married, and he and his wife alone occupied the little cottage, where they received me most hospitably; but with a proud smile he gave me to understand that his family was about to be increased.

This expectation did not in any way interfere with the activity of Paraskèvi, his better half, who in a few minutes prepared for us a supper, consisting of fresh beans cooked in oil, and of caviar, which I contributed, having tapped my kegs, and thus inaugurated the consumption of their contents. Pandéli's friend was of the party, and we feasted, the four of us, like kings.

We had hardly done supping when we heard a knock at the door.

"It must be the demogérontés,"* said Pandéli.

Sure enough, it was the village demogérontés, who entered, their thick, rough walking-staves in hand. They wished us good evening, and sat on the wooden stools offered them by Paraskèvi; we also sat by them, and we all remained silent. I was anxious the conversation should begin, that I might learn the object of their visit; but no one said a word, and the expression of those around me did not convey any feeling of satisfaction. At length the elder of the demogérontés broke the silence.

"Who is this man you have brought here, Pandéli? You are heaping coals upon our heads! It is better he should perish alone, than that we should all be lost!"

These words of the old man filled me with dismay; but Pandéli took up my cause very warmly, saying I was a poor man from

* Aldermen.

Icaria; that I wished only to sell my goods and leave without harming any one; that the Turks would take no notice of me; and much else to the same effect, all of which he gave forth rapidly and with great volubility.

The demogérontés listened to him, shaking their heads like men who would not be convinced. They did not even reply, but they left in silence, and with an anxious look about them. Such was the fear which seized me, lest they should hand me over to the Turks, that I almost decided to abandon my barrels there, forego the object which had brought me to Chio, return by night to the creek, where I hoped to find the caique, and depart. But Pandéli reassured me.

"We will make it all right," he said; "sleep quietly to-night, and we shall see what is to be done to-morrow."

I asked him if he thought it might do any good my offering one tongue of caviar to each of the demogérontés.

"What, gratis!" asked Pandéli, in amazement.

"Well, yes; as a present," I replied.

"In that case, have no fear, Loutzi; they are your men." And he went on to explain to me, at length, how the politics of the village stood. The substance of his long story was that there were two contending parties in the village, each of which took in turn the upper hand by propitiating the Turks, so that the one party was in constant fear of the other. Now, Pandéli did not belong to the party of demogérontés who paid us the visit, but he had no doubt the caviar-tongues would work wonders. The words of Pandéli inspired me with courage, and at the same time sent me to sleep. The fact is I was exhausted by the journey, and, lying down on a horse-hair sack spread on the floor, I was soon fast asleep.

Next morning the sun had hardly risen when the demogérontés again knocked at the door and entered the cottage, silent and demure as before. But I had forestalled them, having got up early, and the caviar-tongues were quite ready, neatly wrapped up in fresh cabbage leaves. My present caused them the greatest satisfaction, and their ways towards me at once changed. They surrounded me, smiling benignantly, and patting me on the back with a patronising air.

Have no fear, Lutzi, they said. You are one of ours. We would rather die than see you suffer.

Although Pandéli had foretold to me the effects of my present, yet I was filled with indignation and disgust. Yesterday they threatened to sacrifice me; to-day, for the sake of a little caviar, they are ready to sacrifice themselves on my behalf! But I dissimulated, and, having expressed to them my gratitude, I asked leave to vend my goods. This they at once accorded me, and having improvised a pair of scales, I set up with my two kegs in the village green and commenced business.

The following day the demogérontés ordered me to accompany them to Kataraktes, a village a few hours' distance from ours, and the seat of a Turkish Agha.

Having other business which took them there, they thought it advisable I should go with them, so as to get the permit of my sojourn confirmed, and thus prevent any accusations on the part of the opposite faction. This measure coincided with my plans, my object being to proceed gradually towards our town.

The demogérontés promised to obtain from the Agha an authorisation enabling me to go about the villages as a trader, and Pandéli readily consented to accompany me as soon as I returned with the permit. We therefore set off, the demogérontés on their asses and I on foot, and arrived at Kataraktes in front of the Agha's conak. They went upstairs, leaving me at the door to look after the asses.

Whilst I stood there waiting, I saw a Turk approach, armed from head to foot. Now I had not come near a Turk since the day we left our home at Chio, nor had I seen one, even from a distance, after those four whose gunshots had accompanied our escape from the island. The sight of this armed man, who came nearer and nearer, suddenly brought back to my recollection our troubles at Smyrna, the long agony of our flight, and the death of Adriana. All this rushed through my memory as the accumulated reminiscences of a whole lifetime crowd back upon the mind of a drowning man. A double feeling of hate and fear took possession of me, and I gazed motionless on that ferocious Turk as he approached.

He addressed to me abruptly some question which I did not understand, and I did not reply. He cast upon me a savage look, and with a loathsome oath he entered the conak. I was fortunate enough not to see his odious face again.

Time went on, however, and I grew impatient, waiting for the demogérontés. At length they came downstairs, but they were not alone. They were accompanied by a Turk, a priest, and a young peasant, who journeyed with us back to the village. The priest and the Turk procured asses before starting, but the young peasant and I walked on foot. I wished to inquire what had been decided with regard to myself, and why our party had so increased in numbers, but the Turk's presence hindered me. He was called Moulah Moustapha. He was a Cretan and spoke Greek, but he did not say much, as it would not be dignified for him, a Turk, to be on familiar terms with the rest of us, who followed him in a line, one after the other.

I, by order of the demogérontés, walked at the side of his ass, by way of servant. The Moulah addressed me only once. He remarked on the wayside a trench full of wild flowers, and he ordered me to fetch for him a particular one which he pointed out with his finger, and called it by its Turkish name. As I did not quite understand which was the one he meant, I cut several flowers from inside the trench, and I ran to catch up the convoy, which had proceeded on its way. I offered to him humbly the bouquet

I had gathered, but unfortunately it did not contain the particular flower which had attracted the attention of the Moulah.

"The one I pointed out is not here, you blockhead! Where do you come from?"

"From Icaria."

"That is why you are stupid; you are not a Chiot."

The flattering allusion to my country consoled me for the poor opinion the Turk had formed of me personally, but, above all, I was pleased with the unexpected mildness of his manner.

When we reached the village I ascertained the reason of the Moulah's presence. He wished to wed forcibly the young man who accompanied us to a young peasant girl, whose protection the Moulah had apparently good reasons for assuming. The young man, being obdurate, had been imprisoned, and the demogérontés interceded in his favour. But the Agha declared for the marriage and, therefore, the Moulah had come with the unfortunate bridegroom and the priest in order to celebrate the ceremony. This was paternal government with a vengeance, and yet this incident bespoke progress. The difficulty was solved neither at the edge of the sword, nor by shutting up the girl in a harem. The Moulah was a kind-hearted man. Let us be fair, and allow to everyone his due.

But with regard to myself—what was the decision arrived at? I was informed that I should have to go to Tholo-Potami for the desired permit. There the chief Agha resided, and the demogérontés intended to visit him in two days.

Two days later, therefore, we again set out. This time our party was more numerous; for the demogérontés brought away with them a load of wine as a present to the Agha, and I was accompanied on my journey by Pandéli, who took with him his ass laden with one of my kegs. The other, which was half empty by this time, remained in charge of Paraskévi as reserve stock.

After five hours' march we reached Tholo-

Potami, but the far-sighted Pandéli did not deem it prudent that we should allow the caviar to come within eye-shot or smelling distance of the Agha or his Turkish surrounding. He therefore remained with the ass outside the village, in the hut of a peasant friend of his, where we arranged he should wait for me. I accompanied the demogérontés into the village. No sooner had we penetrated into its narrow lanes than I was seized with horror at the sight of marks left by the Turks when they had passed through. Then for the first time I beheld the effects of the catastrophe which had come over the island. Till then I had been flying before the devastation. I had felt the storm raging behind me, but I had not yet followed its traces.

A year almost had elapsed since the Turks hurled themselves on Tholo-Potami, but the ruin they had worked seemed still fresh. The shutters of the windows and the doors were either gone or broken, and hung loosely on their hinges. On many walls were to be seen the marks of bullets and the sinister black blotches of fire, while the white walls of one of the houses was still besmeared with the blood which seemed to have flown lavishly from the balcony above. Who can tell the horrible scene of woe and carnage which that balcony must have witnessed! Here and there, amidst ruined and deserted homes, there were a few houses to be seen, the inhabitants of which, still lingering about, had tried to repair some of the ruin they had suffered. But the whole aspect of the village spoke of the fearful havoc which had befallen it, and served as an ample explanation of the abject fear in which our poor demogérontés stood of the Turks.

Their village had so far remained intact. But how could they be easy as to the future? Had not Tholo-Potami itself escaped the first onslaught of the Turks? When two years before they had overrun the island, and had devastated it completely, they had spared, or rather had forgotten, this southern corner of it. The peasants thought the danger was now over, and that the butchers were surfeited with the tribute of blood and gore they had so cruelly extorted from the island. But they deceived themselves miserably. When Kanari's torch avenged the first horrors of Chio, and the air resounded with the explosion of the flagship; when the sea was covered with Turkish corpses, and the Capitan Pacha, half-scorched, expired on the beach, renewed frenzy seized the Turks, and they rushed bodily on the defenceless peasants of the Mastichochoria, there to dip their swords again to the hilt in the blood of innocent victims.

When we arrived in front of the house of the chief Agha, the demogérontés went in, and I remained outside in the street, as at Kataraktes before — I waited, and pondered over what I had witnessed, being especially impressed with that blood-besmeared wall under the balcony.

Presently they called me upstairs into the hall, where the Agha was seated. To his right and left squatted more Turks — his councilmen and assessors—and at the far end of the hall the demogérontés and some other Christians were kept standing by the door.

I bowed my head humbly before the majesty of the Agha. He asked me, through his interpreter, whence I came?

"From Icaria."

"How did I come?"

"On board a caique."

"What did I want now?"

"Permission to vend my goods in the villages."

Thereupon an armed negro approached the Agha, his hand on his breast, and his head bent to the ground.

"Agha," said he, "this young man wears shoes of a Frankish cut. He must be a spy."

And he pointed with his black finger to my feet. The eyes of all, myself included, were turned towards my shoes. In fact, my bluchers were not the shoes of a peasant. I had bought them at Tinos, and had cut away the flaps, thinking that would suffice to complete my disguise. Unfortunately I had not foreseen that their shape could betray me, nor had I then any thought I might ever be taken for a spy.

"Take him to prison!" growled the Agha.

Before I had time to utter a single word the negro had seized me by the arm, and without further ado, without examining into the suspicions aroused by my accursed shoes, he led me to a narrow hole, half lit up through a skylight. He thrust me in by the shoulders, and shut the door. All this was done in an instant—so rapidly, so unexpectedly—that I felt bewildered when I found myself in prison. I hardly knew what had come to me. I could still feel on my shoulders and arms the heavy clutch of the negro; I could hear the angry order of the Agha; I could even recollect the shop, the very face, of my Tiniote shoemaker; and in the darkness of my cell I at first fancied I was dreaming. As soon, however, as my eyes became accustomed to obscurity, I discovered I was not alone. There were with me in that cell two peasants, seated on the floor, and their presence consoled me. There are moments when we long for solitude, but, as a rule, we seek after and desire the society of our-fellow-creatures.

They were father and son, my two companions, and their crime consisted in selling mastic. Half of the total produce of the island was then retained for the use of the sultan's harems, and the peasants might sell the remainder to no one but the Agha, who fixed the price he himself thought fit, and paid it as he pleased, and when he pleased.

The old man spoke first, inquiring who I was, and why I had been imprisoned, and he volunteered his own story. The young man said nothing, but wept silently. His father held him by the hand, and every now and then interrupted his narrative in order to comfort and console the poor lad.

The sight of those two men shook my heart with pain. I thought of my own father and his deserted grave at Spetzæ; of my mother and sisters, who waited for my return at Tinos; and the anguish of my heart rose up and flooded my eyes with tears; and I lamented my fate, and sobbed bitterly. I was in mortal fear of the Turks; they had imprisoned me as a spy without examining me. They might just as easily put me to death. Of what consequence to them was the life of a Giaour? My unfortunate mother was right in dissuading me. Why did I come to Chio at all?

Towards the evening they gave us some bread and olives, and shortly afterwards the negro came, and, leading me out of the cell, took me to the foot of a kiosk in the garden. There, around a low table loaded with fruit of all kinds, sat two Turks and two Christians. Amongst them I recognised the Moulah Moustapha, and the sight of him gave me courage, for he had not impressed me as a harsh man during our last journey.

They began to question me afresh, who I was, whence I came, and what I wanted? I repeated my previous answers, in corroboration of which I tried to invoke the testimony of the Moulah.

"Agha," said I, "did you not see me?"...

The Moulah turned his face away from me; evidently he did not wish to recognise me. I now endeavoured to change the drift of my remarks, but I became confused, and this only confirmed the idea which the protector of the peasant girl had formed of me from the moment I had executed so clumsily his orders about the flower.

"My friends," said he to his hosts in Turkish, "he is not fit for a spy, this mannikin; he is not sharp enough for that. He is an imbecile, the poor devil!"

And they went on talking of me in an undertone, so that I could not make out what they said. The negro presently pushed me out of the kiosk, and led me back to prison. That night and the following one were certainly not of the pleasantest I have ever passed.

Next day the two peasants were taken out of prison and did not return, so that I now remained alone and desolate, counting the hours as they went on, deploring my ill-luck, and wondering what had become of Pandéli and his ass.

The following morning the negro again brought me before the Agha, and I walked into his presence, sad and weary. There was but one hope left—my reputation as one weak in mind, and I was determined to avail myself of it to the utmost, as of a last plank of salvation. The Agha sat smoking his narghillah, surrounded, as usual, by his retinue. The drogman stood by his side, with his arms folded on his breast.

"Bow down before the Agha," he said to me—"He lets you free, but on condition you go towards the town; not roam among the villages whence you came."

I inclined myself low to the earth, kissed the hem of the Agha's garment, and then retreated a few steps backwards. But I thought of Pandéli and my barrels, and of the little creek, whence I hoped to find means to return to Tinos.

"What is he standing there for with his mouth open?" asked the Agha.

"Agha," said I, "I left my shirt in the village, and I must go and fetch it."

The Turk did not understand what I said, and inquired of his drogman. When my prayer was explained to him, he burst out into a loud laugh.

"Very well, very well," said he; "they will fetch your shirt for you. But you must go on to the town."

I bowed again and retired. At the door the negro was waiting for me, and he held out his hand haughtily.

"The prison money," said he.

I had quite forgotten that the imprisoned were liable to the payment of such a tax. I pulled out of my pocket the bag, in which I had a few piastres—the produce of the sale of my caviar—and began untying the knots with evident displeasure. But the knots were many and intricate, and my fingers did not get through the process swiftly enough; so that the negro lost all patience, or perhaps he felt some pity for me, and lifting up his hand, he brought it down heavily on my neck, and after complimenting me with a few words, not of the most affectionate leave taking, he disappeared.

I was now free, and the door being open, I ran out without loss of time, making straight for the village gate. But I found it shut, and no one there. It was Sunday, and all good Christians were at church. My first impulse was to go in also, and thank God for my deliverance; but the desire to get out of Tholo-Potami and look for Pandéli was stronger. I therefore made the sign of the cross there, as I stood under the open sky, I climbed on a tree which grew by the gate, jumped over the wall, and in another instant I was outside the village, feeling once more free and light of heart.

I ran direct to the hut where Pandéli had promised to wait for me. Two days and two nights had elapsed since then. Was it likely he would still be there? I found the hut closed. I knocked at the door, and called out, "Pandéli! Pandéli!" but there was no reply. Behind the hut was the stable; I moved the latch, I walked in, and, joy of joys! I saw Pandéli's ass there, waiting patiently.

Do not laugh, my good reader. I put my arms round his neck and kissed him. I concluded that his pious master was at church. Pandéli had not abandoned me. Soon I saw him return, and I need not attempt to describe our mutual joy at finding ourselves again together.

X.

We were not long settling our itinerary, and starting on our journey. We directed our steps northwards, going from village to village. The sale of the caviar progressed admirably, and the contents of my pouch gradually swelled.

When at length, having reached the heights which shut in the plain, and catching thence a distant glimpse of the town, I tried to fix on the slope of the hills opposite the spot where our tower stood, I felt my heart sink within me, and my knees quiver. I sat on the rocks, and looked upon the green valley below, beaming under the rays of the morning sun. Amidst the trees I could see the houses which studded the plain, but from their chimneys there arose no smoke. To the right, at about half-an-hour's distance, the monastery of Saint Minas was situated. It could not be seen from where we stood, but neither did I wish to go near its charred walls. I sought for no fresh emotions at Chio; I only wished to accomplish the object of my journey, and to leave as quickly as possible. I felt no desire to linger over the devastation of my country; nor did I wish to set eyes on the Turks again.

Pandéli sat near me, enjoying his frugal breakfast, and his ass was busy farther on, searching for food among the scanty bushes on that stony crest. The appetite my two companions had developed provoked mine also. Pandéli's bread and olives, and, above all, the innate cheerfulness of his simple heart, restored my drooping spirits. In a few minutes we started again on our march.

The village of Neochori, where we halted on our descent from the hill, still bore, as did Tholo-Potami, ample evidence testifying to the passage of the Turks through it. But the houses, which had been repaired, were comparatively more numerous, and the devastation appeared at first sight less complete. The coffee-house where we sat to rest ourselves was well filled with men. There was neither an Agha nor a garrison in the place, so that the peasants led a somewhat more comfortable existence, endeavouring to forget in the quietness of to-day the terrors of yesterday, and the probable dangers of the morrow.

My intention was that we should remain at Neochori two or three days, so that I might there settle my plans, but while in the coffee-house I learned news which made me modify my resolutions. From the conversation of the peasants I gathered that a Turkish squadron had anchored at Tchesmé, and that in a few days more ships were expected to arrive from Constantinople, when the combined fleet was to sail against the Greeks.

Evidently I ought to hasten my departure. The Turks on the sea were like the Turks on land; and woe betide those unarmed ships, the passengers in them, and their crews, who fell into their hands. They paid for the victories of Miaoulis and Kanaris, and served to form the lying trophies with which the Turkish admirals covered their shame. To such trophies I had not the least inclination to contribute, nor did I care that my body should decorate the yard-arms of a Turkish flagship. I therefore wished to return to Tinos by all possible means before the enemy's fleet had set sail. I called Pandéli away, and we left the coffee-house. The ass with the keg of caviar stood outside, tied to a post.

"Pandéli," said I, "you remain here to sell the caviar and wait for me. I must leave you."

"Where are you going?"

"I wish to have a look at our tower. To-morrow morning I shall be back."

Pandéli tried to dissuade me; he then offered to accompany me; he reminded me of my imprisonment at Tholo-Potami; but to no purpose. We arranged in what part of the village I should meet him next day; I bought a spade, so as to have the appearance of a labourer in quest of employment, and I took leave of him. He, poor fellow, was uneasy and full of fears; but I felt light of heart; I had the presentiment of success.

As I was making for the village gate, with the spade on my shoulder, I saw, standing by an open door, a man dressed in a half Frankish dress, and smoking. I recognised him from a distance. It was Zenakis, my father's old friend. His hair had grown more gray, and his expression was more solemn than ever. His presence at Neochori surprised me at first, but I recollected that he had estates there.

I went past in front of him, and he took no notice of me. How on earth could he recognise the son of his old friend disguised as a peasant. As I was passing, I hesitated whether I should make myself known to him or not. Better not, thought I, and I continued my walk. But all at once I repented. All the incidents of our residence at Chio rushed back to my mind—how we expected to see him at home every evening; how my father enjoyed his company—and I felt a wish to shake the old gentleman by the hand, and tell him that his good friend was dead. I retraced my steps and stood before him. He stopped smoking, and looked at me in wonderment.

"I should like to say two words to you in private, good sir."

"Come in, my lad; what is it?"

And he went into the courtyard. I followed him, and shut the door behind us.

"Don't you know me?"

"No. Who are you?"

On hearing my name, he lifted up his hands in surprise; he looked at me steadily for a moment, and then seizing me by the hand he embraced me, and drew me aside into his room. I never expected that the heart of that frigid old man was capable of all the tenderness he then showed me. He asked me what had become of us—how we escaped; and I related to him the details of our flight and our errant existence, my father's death, and the sojourn of my widowed mother and sisters at Tinos. He then inquired as to the cause of my return, and I confided to him my projects. He was surprised at my recklessness and my disregard of the danger of the enterprise; he urged me to abandon it, and return whence I came. And when I told him my resolve was firm and not to be shaken, he lifted up his shoulders and smiled.

I got up and took leave of him. He gave me his blessing, and, embracing me, he conducted me to the door. Before letting me out, he put his hand on my shoulder and again tried to persuade me to forget the buried treasure and leave Chio. But the difficulty had been to get to the point I had already reached. How could I now return without so much as casting a parting look on our tower.

"You have made up your mind, and there is an end of it," said the old man with distress. "You are the son of your father, indeed. No more would he listen to reason. Go! . . . If you get into trouble with the Turks," he added in a milder tone, "let me know. As a consul I have some influence, and I may be of use to you. God be with you!"

And he opened the door. The sun was now setting, and the distance to our tower was still about two hours' walk. I quickened my step, wishing to get there before nightfall. My polar star was the well-known little hill and the trees which hid from view our chapel on its crest. I walked on rapidly with the spade on my shoulder, and my mind was busy at work. I was thinking especially of the future. Being confident I should find the two sacks, I was considering how to dispose of the gold and silver plate, and I planned how, with the proceeds, I should repair with my mother and sisters to Italy—perhaps to England, and what sort of business I should organise. My fancy was already conjuring up pictures of future happiness. But as I approached, and the evening shadows spread over the country, a confused feeling of anxiety began to take possession of me. Why did I come alone? Why did I not allow Pandéli to accompany me?

I had considered it more prudent not to take him with me, fearing lest I should arouse suspicions had I appeared in that neighbourhood with my companion and his ass. Alone, I could more easily conceal myself, and watch a favourable moment to penetrate into the garden. As for the sacks, I intended hiding them in the wood near the chapel, and next day to pass that way with Pandéli and take them. But now I repented, and wished I had Pandéli with me. My courage wavered as the moment for action approached. But it was too late. I was already outside the wall of our garden, and from the road I could see the upper part of our house. There was the window of my bedroom; there the two windows of my father and mother's room; there . . . but why were the windows trelissed? Was I mistaken?—No! . . . It is my home, but now inhabited by Turks! And I wandering in the high roads, I look upon its walls as an outcast, and watch its windows like a thief.

I wished to see better, to satiate my eyes with the sad sight of my estrangement and bereavement. I jumped over the hedge opposite our garden wall, and went up the vineyard which the road separated from the garden. The ground was steep at this point, so that from it I could look over the whole of our estate. In the house and around it there was not a soul to be seen; but in the garden an old gardener was hard at work digging. I at once recognised his figure. It was our own gardener, old Yanni, whose daughter I had discovered in the service of Mavroyenis at Tinos.

My joy on recognising him was great. Nor was my satisfaction devoid of egotism, for I thus secured a trusty auxiliary in my attempt, and I had ready for the old man an acceptable recompense for his assistance —the good tidings that his daughter was alive and safe. But how communicate with him? I dare not call him, nor enter the garden. Should I wait till nightfall, and then go stealthily to his hut, present myself to him, and claim his assistance? But until then . . .

The sun was now hid behind the distant hills, but the limpid sky still reflected an abundant twilight. It was a delightful summer's evening; all was calm and serene, and everything in the plain seemed so happy under the trees. Nature does not suffer when we are in pain. Its very serenity increases the sorrow of the troubled heart.

I descended from the vineyard into the road, and went towards the chapel, my head bent down, as if trying to trace on the dust the footsteps of those with whom I had so often walked there. I was still at some distance from the wood surrounding the chapel, when I saw emerge from amongst the trees female forms, and children running around them. They came towards me as I was walking up the hill, but I was no longer in time to recede, when I discovered they were Turkish women. A black eunuch accompanied them, and his trailing mantle did not easily distinguish him at a distance from the forms of the women.

I stood aside as the harem passed on, and the children followed, playing amongst themselves the while. One of these, however, a girl of about twelve years, did not mix with the others, but walked quietly, last of all, holding flowers in one hand, the other arm hanging listlessly by her side. Passing by, she stood and looked up at me as I went on my way.

Suddenly I heard behind me a little voice whisper my name—" Louki!" Before I had time to think that if I turned round I would betray myself, and if found out I was a lost man, I looked back, and saw the little girl standing at a few paces from me. The other children had gone on. As soon as she saw me turn round, she knelt on the ground. I recognised her at once. I all but cried out Despina! But she put her fingers to her lips, and, looking at me, she whispered, "Louki, save me!" and then stooping down, she pretended to gather flowers, for she had already heard the hoarse voice of the eunuch, who turned back to gather in his flock. Despina got up and ran on to the other children, and I, hiding behind the trees, followed the group of figures from a distance, till I saw the Negro open the door of our garden and let in the women and children. Last of all Despina entered, and, before passing through the door, she turned and looked back; she felt sure I followed her steps. The eunuch went in after her, and the door was again closed.

I sat under the trees, my head buried in my hands, and I endeavoured to collect my thoughts. Despina in the hands of the Turks! She a slave in our own tower! And how she recognised me, as if she had expected me! Her supplicating voice re-echoed in my ears. "Save me, Louki!" This was the mysterious power which attracted me to Chio. It was for this that Providence guided me there. I shall save her! But how?... And I considered one plan after another.

Night had now approached, but darkness was not yet complete. The moon had still two hours to run on her slow course before she disappeared behind the hill, and the sky above us was lit up with her brilliancy. Her rays coquetting with the leaves of the trees, formed on the ground, where I sat, thousands of fantastic devices. I gazed upon these varying shadows, I heard the barking of the dogs in the distant farms, and nearer me the chirping of the crickets, mingled with the harsher croaking of the frogs. But my thoughts were fixed elsewhere; I heard, but did not listen; yet my mind was impressed with those echoes of the serene night, with the perfume offered up by the flowers, and with the play of the moonlight through the branches of the trees.

As soon as the moon had set, and darkness spread over the country, I rose; I invoked the help of God, and advanced into the road. I walked without hesitation, for I had made up my mind; I knew what was my aim—my plans had been fixed. I went forth to carry it out, and God would help me.

The darkness was now complete, but I remembered every inch of the ground, so that I could find my way about even with my eyes shut. Reaching the corner where the garden wall became lower, I jumped over it, and I was inside the garden. I stood motionless by the wall, lest the sound of my leap had been heard. There was complete stillness. Not a dog's growl, not a human voice, to be heard. Only a few steps separated me from the gardener's hut. The door was closed, but after a turn of the latch, I found myself inside it. How often in my younger days had I visited old Yanni there, and how often he set me on his knee, and satisfied my greediness with the choicest fruits of his labours! The little room was dark, but I could hear the sonorous breathing of the old man. I walked on tiptoe towards him, fearing lest he should awake before recognising me, and I wished to avoid startling him. I knelt near him, and, stooping down, I pronounced his name.

"Yanni, Yanni, it is I, Louki. Don't be alarmed. I, Louki."

The old man awoke, holding his breath, but he neither moved nor said a word. Perhaps he thought he was dreaming. I put my hand on his arm, and again pronounced my name. He sat up on his bed, but some time passed before he could quite collect his thoughts. He then tried to light a candle. But I prevented him, and our conversation was continued in the dark. He trembled with joy when he heard that his daughter was alive at Tinos, and that we would return there together. I then explained to him why I had come, and I asked him to assist me.

He at once got up, dressed hurriedly, and opened the door of the hut. Before stepping out, I took hold of his arm.

"Who lives in our tower, Yanni?"

"The harem of Nejib-Agha."

"Who is Nejib-Agha?"

"One of the chiefs of the Anatolians, who have ravaged the land."

"And does he not live here?"

"They expect him to-morrow."

"Has he any Christian women in his harem?"

"Only Kalani's daughter."

"And Kalani, what has become of him?"

"The Turks murdered him."

Despina's lament when we followed our parents to the chapel flashed back to my mind—"They will kill my father. The Turks kill. They will kill him!" Her presentiment did not deceive her; her father was slaughtered, while mine was laid to rest in the deserted grave at Spetzæ!

We left the hut, and silently crept towards the corner of the garden, where the apple-tree stood. I showed the spot to the old man. I remembered it well. I could have fancied I still saw my father dig in front of me, with the two sacks lying on the edge of the trench. The spade of the old gardener hit the earth heavily, and the thud resounded through the garden.

"Gently, gently, Yanni, lest they hear us."

"Have no fear; it will not matter if they do. They will think I am preparing the ditches for watering."

The old man continued digging; and I also set to work near him, opening up the trench with my spade. As my arms rose and fell, I fancied that a tender voice re-echoed in my ears, "Louki, save me!" Every dig of the spade repeated in the same voice, "Louki, Louki!"

Suddenly we heard the clash of metal. I jumped into the trench, and began to throw up the earth with my hands. The gardener's spade had torn the sack asunder, but I lifted it carefully, and placed it at the root of the apple-tree. The other sack lay under the first. I took it up and laid it next its fellow, and we filled up the trench carefully.

"And now?" asked Yanni.

"Now the sacks on our shoulders and away!"

"Where are we going?"

"To Neochori."

"It is a long way, and it is very dark."

"So much the better, Yanni; no one will see us."

"But how enter into Neochori with the sacks on our shoulders? and, besides, that one is torn. The things in it may fall out. Wait!"

After a few minutes' absence, Yanni returned with two large baskets, in each of which he placed one of the sacks. He filled them up with cabbages and other vegetables, and taking one each on our shoulders, we set off on our march.

It was just dawning when we reached Neochori, and we sat on a low fencing wall awaiting the morning. I was exhausted. My shoulders and arms ached with the weight of so unusual a load. But I did not think of fatigue and pain. One thought alone dominated my mind, only one desire possessed my heart, and for that I felt I could brave anything. I wished to save that orphan child, who had appealed to me.

As soon as the sun had risen, we again

took up our baskets, and continued our march. We found no difficulty in penetrating into the village, and we made straight for Zenakis' house. The dear old gentleman could not hide his joy at seeing me enter his courtyard again.

"Welcome, my boy!" he said. "So you have succeeded, and without any mishap!"

And seeing Yanni following behind me, he asked me who he was. I told him he was our gardener.

"You have offered me your assistance," I added; "and I claim it now."

"What is it? Did any one see you? Are the Turks after you?"

"No; but Turks occupy our tower, and a Christian girl is there a slave, whose father was a family friend of ours. The child saw me, recognised me, appealed to me, and I must save her."

"How can you save her? Do you by any chance propose carrying her away?"

"I propose to ransom her," I replied.

"And where is the money to come from?

The Turks sell human flesh dear, especially when it is tender."

"I have no money, but I have these sacks, which God has helped me to recover."

"But these things do not belong to you alone. They are your mother's also, and your sisters'. Your father did not hide them for you to dispose of at your pleasure."

"I have considered the matter well before deciding; but I feel sure I am not doing anything distasteful to my father's soul in thus applying the heritage he has left, and that from my mother I shall hear blessings, not complaints. As for my sisters, I have my trust in God that he will help me to secure for them a richer dowry than their portion of these things."

"Then you are decided to sacrifice even the whole of them."

"The whole, if it be necessary."

The expression of Zenakis' face showed he did not condemn my decision by any means. He asked me for more particulars as to Despina, and he desired to see how far the contents of the sacks were likely to satisfy the avidity of the Turk. He therefore showed us upstairs into his bedroom. There we emptied the sacks, and the floor was strewn with spoons, large and small, trays, cups, and other gold and silver objects, such as made up the luxury of those days, when houses were not crammed with the showy but flimsy finery of Paris and Vienna. These products now crowd tables and burthen sideboards for show, not for use. Then ornaments were few, but valuable and substantial; and descending from father to son, they constituted a veritable fund, and an available resource in the hour of need.

I begged Zenakis to press on the negotiations with the Agha, so that I might manage to leave Chio before the Turkish fleet set sail. But the old gentleman would not hurry, and tried to repress my impatience. Yet, under that cold and demure aspect, a warm heart lay hid. And while he rebuked and twitted me, he had ordered his mule, and in a few minutes he started for the tower.

As soon as he had left I went to look for Pandéli. His protracted absence from home began to disturb the good peasant. His thoughts were constantly with his wife.

"What must Paraskévi think of it all?" he said. "She must consider us as lost."

"Never you mind, Pandéli. I promise you we shall be back to-morrow morning, and Paraskévi will be satisfied. I will make a present to her of the rest of my unsold caviar as a first settlement on the heir she promises you."

How slowly the hours of that morning passed! I spent the best part of the day in Zenakis' garden, at the back of his house, passing up and down, trying to figure to myself what was being said at that moment in our tower, and how the negotiations for the ransom of Despina progressed. What Zenakis would say I could easily guess; but how would the Turk reply? Would he strike the bargain, or would he prefer to keep the Christian girl as a future ornament of his harem? And my cheeks flushed with anger, and I got up, and sat down, full of uneasiness. Every sound in the house, each voice in the street, seemed to me to be connected with Despina's redemption.

At length Zenakis returned, and not alone. I heard him talk in Turkish. Who could it be that accompanied him? Was it the Agha, or had he brought Despina? I hid myself in the trees opposite the window of the room where the child's ransom was ranged out in order. I heard Zenakis and the Turk converse, but I could not make out what they said. All at once I see them approach the window. The Agha, a stately looking Turk, balanced in his hand a tray, as if trying to ascertain its probable weight; while Zenakis called his attention to other pieces of plate which he held in both his hands.

My hopes were revived. The Turk examined the things; consequently he did not reject the bargain.

They both withdrew from the window, and I heard our host's voice ordering coffee, and shortly afterwards I heard the street door open and Zenakis take leave of the Agha. The door was again shut, but I remained motionless; I dared not ask what was the result.

Zenakis came to look for me in the garden.

"We have settled the matter, Louki," he said. "He is gone to fetch the child. We will have her here this evening."

I threw myself on his neck and I embraced him, crying. Why did I weep? Does the heart know why it palpitates? Can the innermost feelings of the soul be analysed? I had not gone to Chio on Despina's account; but while I was there waiting till her captor fetched her, I fancied my whole life was centred in her. I did not think of the treasure, nor of the plans I had made contingent on its recovery. I thought only of the joy with which I would conduct the orphan girl into the arms of my mother.

Towards evening the Agha returned, bringing Despina with him, and he went back alone with Yanni's two baskets on his mule. After he had left, Zenakis called me into his room. Despina flew towards me. She wished to speak, but she could only pronounce my name: "Louki, Louki," and tears streamed from her eyes. I held out to her my hands, and pressed her to my bosom; but I did not kiss her. I dared not.

That same evening we left Neochori along with Yanni. Pandéli's ass carried Despina disguised as a peasant boy, for security's sake. Paraskévi received us with open arms, and, thanks to her husband's exertions, we found in the very creek where Kephala had landed me, a boat, in which we embarked the next evening, and, under a fair wind, we arrived safely at Tinos the day after.

My mother's joy when she saw me return was indescribable. Her tears of gladness on that occasion were the measure of the grief she had experienced during my absence.

"I have not brought you your gold and your silver plate, dear mother. But here is what I have brought to you." And so saying, I pushed Despina into her arms.

I knew it was to a mother's embrace I was taking the unhappy orphan.

I resumed at once my operations, and having carried out my project of the association, which had been checked for a time, I repaired to Syra and soon brought over there our family. God blessed my labours. I endowed and married my sisters to my partners, and four years after my last departure from Chio I was wedded to Despina, with the consent and blessing of my mother.

Some time afterwards I left with her and established myself in England.

Our life has since passed in happiness. But never, in the midst of prosperity, have I forgotten the trials of my youth. Often, when I see my daughters and grandchildren decked out in their toilets, and my wife dressing her white hair in the last fashion of

Europe, I remind her of the trousers she had to wear when I carried her away in disguise on Pandéli's ass, and we both laugh, and from the depths of our hearts thank Almighty God.

NOTES.

THE following extract from Th. Gordon's *History of the Greek Revolution* (London, 1832, vol. i. p. 35), may serve as an introduction into these Notes, elucidating as it does much to which they refer :—" The thirty years that elapsed from 1790 to 1820, made, in the ideas and prospects of the Greeks, a wonderful alteration, proceeding chiefly from two causes; the growing influence acquired by Russia in Eastern affairs after the peace of Yassy, and the consequences of the French Revolution. The first afforded them hopes of future liberation, as well as ready means of exchanging obedience to Ottoman authority, individually, for the protection of the Court of St. Petersburg, through the medium of the Russian Embassy at Constantinople. The second, by creating a demand for corn in the ports of the west, sharpened their instinctive love of commerce and navigation, and, for a paltry coasting traffic in small barks, substituted strong and lofty vessels, distant voyages, and extensive speculation. By unlocking the straits between the Euxine and the Mediterranean, the Empress Catherine had procured an outlet for the harvests of Poland and Southern Russia. The new town of Odessa, built on a Tartarian steppe, attracted a multitude of Greeks, all occupied in commercial pursuits. War had paralysed the merchant marine in France; while that of Austria, now so flourishing, did not as yet exist. Thus the trade of the Black Sea fell, without competition, into the hands of some islanders of the Ægean. The impulse, once given, was followed up with singular alacrity; at Constantinople, Smyrna, Salonika, and every great city of the Turkish Empire; at Odessa, Trieste, Leghorn, and all the principal ports of Europe, were established opulent Greek houses, whose rising prosperity casting into shade that of the foreign Levant merchants, excited too commonly in the breasts of the latter a rancorous feeling of hostility, which has been its own punishment."

PAGE 4.

"Of all the Ottoman provinces, that, sheltered by special privileges, prospered under and in spite of Oriental despotism, the most flourishing and beautiful was Chios. That island, 30 miles in length, 12 in breadth, and separated from the shore of Ionia by a strait of 7 miles, contained a large and well-built city, 68 villages, 300 convents, 200 churches, and a population of 100,000 Greeks, 6000 Turks, and a small number of Catholics and Jews. Its capital, situated on the eastern side, and at an equal distance from the northern and southern extremities, was remarkable for the beauty and solidity of its edifices; 30,000 people resided there, including all the Mohammedans and Israelites. Celebrated for its fertility, and the enchanting aspect of its gardens, Chios carried on a brisk trade in silk and fruit; from thence Constantinople was supplied with oranges, lemons, and citrons; but the most valuable production of the country is gum mastic, expressed from the seed of a species of lentiscus, a substance highly prized by the Eastern ladies, who amuse their indolence by chewing it, deriving from that practice as much gratification as their male relations enjoy by inhaling the fumes of tobacco. As it is peculiar to one district, the 22 villages furnishing mastic were an appanage of the Imperial Harem, while the remaining 46 belonged to the metropolitan Church of Constantinople. The character of the Chians partook of the softness of their climate and the delicacy of the products of their soil. Mild, gay, lively, acute, industrious, and proverbially timid, they succeeded alike in commerce and literature; the females were noted for their charms and grace, and the whole people, busy and contented, neither sought nor wished for a change in their political condition.[1] At Constantinople and Smyrna, thousands of Sciotes found employment as boatmen, gardeners, and handicraftsmen; and there, as in the west, they had established the wealthiest and most considerable Greek commercial houses. Ardent promoters of education, and passionately fond of their native land, the rich citizens, sparing no expense to embellish it, had founded in their town a splendid college, library, museum, printing presses, and hospitals."—*Gordon*, vol. i. p. 350. For a full and faithful description of the municipal and other institutions of Chio, prior to the Revolution, see the excellent work of M. Foustel de Conlanges, *Mémoire sur l'ile de Chio*, Paris, 1857, 8vo.

PAGE 4.

" It would have been long, perhaps, ere they had been able, within their own territory, and

---

[1] This of course refers to the mass living at home; the Sciote merchants settled abroad were generally zealous in the cause of liberty.

under the eye of their masters, to organise a general rising, if the famous association of the Hetæria had not furnished a proper medium of communication, and extended its ramifications into each city, isle, and district, where Greeks were to be met with. The birth of that society is enveloped in mystery. Some persons assert that the ex-hospodar of Wallachia, Alexander Mavrocordato, long an exile in Russia, founded it about the commencement of the present century, with the ostensible view of promoting education; while others give the merit to Riga, and consequently carry its origin farther back. What appears certain is, that, from the epoch of the French Revolution, a few Greeks busied themselves in imagining plans for the liberation of their country. Of this number were Alexander Ypsilanti's father (who privately stirred up and supported with money the Servians) and Anthimos Gazi, a Thessalian, and a distinguished scholar, one of Riga's associates, and editor of a literary journal published at Vienna in the Romaic tongue. It was not, however, until 1815 that the Hetæria assumed form and consistence as a political society, when the Greeks, who had expected that the Congress of Vienna would work a change in Eastern affairs, finding their hopes disappointed in that respect, resolved to take measures for emancipating themselves."—*Gordon*, vol. i. p. 40.

Page 5.

Rhigas, who is considered as "the first martyr" to the cause of Greek liberty, was born at Velestino, in Thessaly, in 1754. Fired at an early age with a thirst for freedom, he quitted his native place, and being possessed of considerable learning, was named in 1790 Secretary to the then Hospodar of Walachia Mavrojenis. His whole energies were now concentrated in organising a movement of national regeneration, entering into communication with the primates in different parts of Greece, and composing stirring patriotic hymns. He had even opened up negotiations with Bernadotte, the French ambassador at Vienna, and on the fall of Venice he proceeded to Trieste, in order personally to explain his project to Bonaparte, and claim his support. But he was arrested by the Austrian authorities, who delivered him to the Pacha of Belgrade in 1798. Every effort to secure his release proved unavailing, and on his offering resistance to his executioners, when led to be drowned in the Danube, he was shot. While dying he said: "I have sown the seed, and the time will come when my countrymen will reap its sweet fruits." His hymns, especially the Δεῦτε παῖδες τῶν Ἑλλήνων and Ὥς ποτε παλληκάρια, became the watchwords of every Greek, and the music to which they were sung was so stirring, that the Turks themselves repeated the first three words, without understanding their significance, whenever they bid their Greek slaves sing them.

PAGE 5.

The better kind of country houses in Chio are called towers. Indeed they are mostly built in that form, the custom having survived the danger of the piratical incursions which first fostered the introduction of this architecture in the times of the Crusaders.

PAGE 8.

Prince Ypsilanti crossed the Pruth on March 7, 1821, and placed himself at the head of the revolted Greeks at Moldavia. News of this reached Constantinople on March 14, and both he and Michael Soutzos, the Hospodar of Walachia, were declared outlaws. On April 4 of the same year, Germanos, the Archbishop of Patræ, unfurled the flag of liberty in the Morea. On the 15th the Spetziotes revolted; on the 22d the island of Psara, and on the 29th Hydra and Samos rose in arms.

PAGE 9.

"As it was thought impossible that Ypsilanti should have engaged in so gigantic an enterprise without hopes of powerful support, the Turks naturally concluded that Russia was at the bottom of the whole affair. . . . Supposing themselves surrounded on every side by open or concealed enemies, ready to extirpate their religion and nation, they saw no security except in the utter destruction of the Greek Rayahs. Under the influence of this feeling, the Janissaries and the populace, both at Constantinople and in the villages on the Bosphorus, began to commit murders, and to break into houses; and as the Porte seemed not simply to tolerate, but rather to countenance such excesses, universal dismay passed into the breasts of the Christians. At the same time, the Sultan, by an imperial rescript, called upon his Mohammedan subjects to gird on their weapons, and stand prepared to defend their faith and monarchy, menaced by infidels; by his orders, too, the Patriarch of the Eastern Church fulminated an excommunication against Ypsilanti and his adherents."—*Gordon*, vol. i. p. 184.

PAGE 11.

The great mass of the Jews in the Turkish Empire were established there on being expelled from Spain by Ferdinand and Isabella, the Catholics; and their familiar idiom is still a mixture of corrupt Spanish with some Greek and Turkish words.

Page 15.

"But it was on the coasts of Asia Minor that the most sanguinary reactions prevailed, and the city of Smyrna was remarkable for the atrocity and duration of its troubles, and the torrents of blood shed there. That great emporium of the Levant trade, situated at the bottom of a spacious gulf, into which the Hermus pours its waters, was supposed to contain 180,000 people, among whom might be reckoned natives of every part of the world. Here, as at Constantinople, reports of Ypsilanti's entering Moldavia produced a fermentation, which gradually augmented, as rumours of a vast conspiracy formed by the Rayahs were transmitted from the capital. A body of recruits arriving from the interior, and quartered round the town, indulged in unbridled license, assassinating the Greek peasants, and threatening to kill all the infidels. For a time, the Janissaries of Smyrna, taking upon themselves the police of the city, and Hassan, Pasha of Cesarea, who came to govern it, maintained a degree of order, interrupted occasionally by single murders, tumults, and panic terrors, sometimes proceeding from trivial causes; thus, on the 11th of April, the discharge of a pistol excited so much alarm, that multitudes rushed to the harbour, and several persons were drowned in their hurry to escape."—*Gordon*, vol. i. p. 190.

PAGE 17.

The islands of Hydra, Spetzæ, and Psara, are specially designated by Greeks as *Naval islands*, owing to the strength and superiority of their navy, which proved of such value to the cause of the insurrection.

PAGE 21.

"On the 16th of April, Prince Constantine Morousi, Dragoman to the Porte, was apprehended, without any previous warning, conducted to a summer-house of the Seraglio, called the Alcikiosk, and there beheaded. Immediately afterwards, ten conspicuous personages of the Fanar (including a brother of Prince Hanjerli, a Mavrocordato, a Scanavi, and Theodore Rizo) were executed, and a similar fate overtook many rich merchants and bankers. The interest that waited upon their deaths, and the simultaneous destruction of a crowd of obscurer victims, was soon absorbed by a deeper sympathy for a more illustrious sufferer. Gregory, the Byzantine Patriarch, a

Peloponnesian by birth, was an aged prelate, of blameless life and manners, whose piety and virtues commanded general esteem; indeed, the high opinion entertained of him, had, during the course of a long life, caused his repeated promotion to the metropolitan throne of the East. As he was leaving his chapel, after the celebration of divine service, on the evening of Easter Sunday (April 22), he was arrested by some Turkish officers, stripped of his pontifical robes, and hanged at the gate of his own palace; his body, left suspended for three days, was then cut down, delivered to a squad of Jews,[1] selected from the lowest rabble, dragged through the streets, and thrown into the sea. Next night, a few zealous Christians fished up the mortal remains of the martyr, and conveyed them to Odessa, where, on the 1st of July, they were interred with solemn pomp. At the instant of the Patriarch's execution, three archbishops (those of Ephesus, Derkos, and Auchialus), and eight priests of a superior order, were put to death in different quarters of the city, and their bodies treated with equal indignity. Gregory's deplorable fate excited

[1] It was by such means that the Porte excited its subject races, the one against the other. A striking contrast to this is now presented by the relations of perfect fellowship existing between the Greeks and their Jewish fellow countrymen in the free kingdom of Greece. To this the Greek Hebrews have given a public attestation.—J. G.

throughout Europe a profound feeling of horror and pity, and exasperated tenfold the animosity of the Greeks, insomuch as to render their reconciliation with the Porte impossible."— *Gordon*, vol. i. p. 187. To the above narrative we may add that fifty years later (in 1871) a steamship under the flag of regenerated Greece traversed the Bosphorus, bearing from Odessa the remains of the Patriarch, which now repose in the Cathedral of Athens.

PAGE 30.

Jacob Tombazi, the first admiral of the united fleets of Hydra, Spetzæ, and Psara, appeared before Chio on May 4th, 1821, but again sailed away on the 19th, without succeeding in raising the islanders to revolt.

PAGE 33.

"As soon as the revolution broke out, the Greek fleet, commanded by Tombazi, appeared before Scio, and disseminated an incendiary proclamation. It is said they might then have seized the castle, the Turks, as well as their Motesellim (governor), being completely panic-struck. Very different, however, from their Samian neighbours, the effeminate Chians, trembled at the idea of danger; the primates besought Tombazi not to compromise their safety, and that step of the Hydriotes served only to alarm the Porte, which despatched there a body of Asiatic and Candiote troops. From that moment there was an end to the peace and happiness of Scio; the soldiers robbed, and even murdered the peasants; and the archbishop and primates, who had vaguely flattered themselves that their isle might rest in neutrality, were imprisoned in the castle as pledges of the people's submission. The number of hostages, not exceeding four at first, was gradually increased to eighty, selected from the most opulent and respectable class, and chiefly fathers of families. They were so closely confined, that some of them died without being allowed to bid adieu to their friends, and one was assassinated in sport by his Moslem guards. Terror, meanwhile, hung over the city and villages, and amidst present suffering from the outrages of their garrison, the Sciotes contemplated the future with shuddering, lest it should heap on them worse misfortunes."— *Gordon*, vol. i. p. 352.

PAGE 37.

The first Turkish line-of-battle ship was burnt by Papa Nicolis on May 27th, 1821. The town of Cydoniæ was completely destroyed by the Turks on the 4th of June (*Gordon*, vol. i. p. 208). On the 8th of July the Turks were on the point of making a descent upon Samos, when the Greek fleet appearing suddenly, burnt nine of the enemy's transports, and thus frustrated his designs. The massacres of Cyprus commenced on the 9th, and continued incessantly for thirty days (*Gordon*, p. 193). Tripolitza was taken by assault by the Greeks on September 23d, 1821. The massacres of Cassandra took place on the 30th of the next October (*Gordon*, p. 287). The same authority describes as follows the massacres of Smyrna:—

"At length the news of a defeat sustained by the Ottoman marine off Lesbos brought fury to a crisis on the 15th of June; on that and the following day 3000 ruffians assailed the Greek quarter, plundered the houses, and slaughtered the people. Smyrna resembled a place taken by assault, neither age nor sex being respected. . . . In these melancholy circumstances, the conduct of the French Consul (Monsieur David) did him high honour; his house and garden being crowded with Greek fugitives, the rabble of assassins was on the point of breaking in, and his Janissaries did not venture to resist; when the Consul, placing himself at the gate with one companion, overawed the incensed Mohammedans by his dignified carriage, until the boats of a French corvette, coming to his assistance, forced the villanous throng to seek some easier prey."—p. 191.

Page 44.

In November 1821 a certain Bournias, a native of Chio, but formerly captain in the regiment of *Chasseurs d'Orient*, raised by the French Republic, and who, on that account, always wore an old French uniform, presented himself at Ypsilanti's headquarters with a project for raising a revolt at Chio. Having met with a cold reception from the Prince, he proceeded to Samos, then under the supreme dictatorship of Lycurgos Logothétes, father of the late learned Archbishop of Syra, Alexander Lycurgos, who was so well known in England.

"On the night of the (10) 22d of March 1822, Logothétes and Bournias, arriving with a flotilla of eight brigs and thirty launches or sakolevas, effected a disembarkation to the south of Scio. Versions differ with regard to the force that accompanied them. It was then stated, in Smyrna, at 5000; later accounts diminished it to 2500, and the most moderate reports make it amount to only 500 Samoans and 150 Chian exiles, with two pieces of cannon; but this last estimate seems altogether inadequate to the number of transports. A corps of several hundred Turks detached against them fled precipitately, supposing itself attacked by 30,000 men, and all the exterior positions being abandoned with equal cowardice, the insurgents, reinforced by a body of peasants, entered the city. The citizens, overwhelmed with consternation, shut themselves up in their houses. However, when, at three hours after noon, the Christian standards were borne through the streets in procession amidst shouts of " Liberty! Liberty!" they from their windows greeted the strangers with a faint and insincere welcome. The villagers, less timid, and provoked at the ill-treatment they had experienced, cordially joined the invaders, with such weapons as they had concealed, or could at the instant procure, their rulers having long before prescribed a general disarming." — *Gordon*, p. 354.

PAGE 60.

Adamantios Korais was born at Smyrna in 1748, his father being one of the many Chiote merchants in that city. Being averse to a commercial career, he studied medicine at Montpelier, and afterwards repaired to Paris, where he resided to his death, in April 1833. By his philological and patriotic writings he stirred up the national idea and greatly contributed to the revival of Greek learning. He is therefore justly considered as the most eminent of modern Greek litterati.

Page 63.

"Expecting hourly the approach of the Sultan's navy, menaced by an army of 30,000 Ottomans assembled on the opposite shore, disguising real terror under a mask of confident resolution, the insurgents were faintly pressing the siege of the castle, when, on the morning of the 11th of April, the Capitan Pasha, Kara Ali, appeared off the island with a fleet of six line-of-battle ships, ten frigates or large corvettes, and twelve smaller vessels of war. The Greek blockading squadrons, which counted fourteen brigs and six schooners, immediately fled; and the grand admiral, stretching his line along the coast, communicated with Vehib Pasha, and obtained precise information respecting the posture of affairs. Indeed, the Greeks left him no room to doubt their intention of braving him; for, on descrying his armament, they redoubled their fire against the citadel, and cannon, placed at intervals along the heights, opened on his ships. A Turkish felucca of two guns and eighty men having got too near the land, struck on a shoal, and almost the whole of its crew was picked off by the enemy's musketry. Kara Ali then ordered a disembarkation, and several thousand men landed under cover of the artillery of his fleet; at the same instant Vehib Pasha made a sortie with his garrison, and a flotilla of boats continually transported troops from the camp of Tchesmè. The Turks rushed into the town, and, after a combat of short duration, carried, sword in hand, the height of Tourlotti and the hostile batteries. The city then displayed a scene which might be amply compared to the sack of Tripolizza. Mercy was out of the question, the victors butchering indiscriminately all who came in their way; shrieks rent the air, and the streets were strewed with the dead bodies of old men, women, and children; even the inmates of the hospital, the madhouse, and the deaf and dumb institution, were inhumanly slaughtered. Flames first bursting from the church of Tourlotti, gave the signal for a general conflagration, which raged the two following days, and devoured one of the finest cities in the Levant. . . . It is thought that 9000 persons of every age and sex were slain at the storming of the town."—*Gordon*, vol. i. p. 357.

Page 63.

" Three thousand Chiots retired to the monastery of Aghios Mynas, which lies five miles to the southward of the city, on the ridge of hills which bounds the rich plain. The Turks surrounded the building and summoned them to surrender. The men had little hope of escaping death. The women and children were sure of being sold as slaves. Though they had no military leader, and were unable to take effectual measures for defending the monastery, they refused to lay down their arms. The Turks carried the building by storm, and put all within to the sword."—Finlay, *History of the Greek Revolution,* vol. i. p. 313.

PAGE 67.

" The Samians alone were able to offer resistance for some time at Hagios-Georgios; but subsequently abandoning the island to the terrible fate they had prepared for it, they took refuge at Psara, where Lykourgos was threatened with proceedings of a capital nature." —Gervinus, *Insurrection et Régénération de la Grèce,* Paris, 1863. Vol. i. p. 368.

PAGE 69.

" In the interior some fighting occurred; and at Vrondado and Thymiana, the insurgents are said to have made an honourable stand. It is not less true, however, that the majority of the Sciotes either suffered themselves to be slain or bound like sheep, or else dragged on a miserable existence in mountains and caverns, seeking an opportunity to escape by sea, as many of them did, in boats that came to their rescue from Psara, Tinos, and other insular ports."—*Gordon*, vol. i. p. 359.

Page 76.

"On the whole of the island of Psara there were but four wells, three of which produced a brackish water. The fourth, situated inside the town, had to suffice for the wants of the inhabitants. The houses had cisterns." *Chroniques du Levant, ou Mémoires sur la Grèce et les contrées voisines.* Paris, Drobb, 1825.

Page 78.

Desirous of preserving the district that furnished mastic to the Seraglio, and satiated with the torrents of blood that flowed for six days, Kara Ali transmitted an application through Vehib Pasha to the English Consul Guidici, the Austrian Consul Stiepevidi, and Monsieur Digeon, agent of France, requesting them to propose an amnesty to the insurgents. . . . . On the 17th they set out on their mission, bearing with them an imperial firman, offering pardon to the Sciotes on their unconditional submission, and a letter signed by Archbishop Plato and the hostages confined in the castle, begging them to surrender at discretion. Owing to the prodigious confusion that prevailed among the troops, Messieurs Digeon and Stiqsevich alone succeeded in reaching the Christian quarters with considerable personal risk; they returned on the 22d, accompanied by the primates of the twenty-two mastic villages, and a train of mules loaded with arms.—*Gordon*, p. 359.

"Malheur à ceux qui, dédaignant l'asile protecteur des navires psariotes sur les côtes, se fièrent à cette guarantie et rentrèrent chez eux! À peine les Turcs se virent-ils certains de leur proie et à l'abri de tout danger, qu' ils se dispersèrent, comme des bêtes féroces qu'on a lâchées, dans toute l'île, se jetant sur le people sans armes, s'attaquant à tous les habitants sans avoir égard à l'âge, ni au sexe, sans distinguer les gens dévoués au sultan des rebelles, et portant, pendant des semaines entières, le meurtre et l'esclavage dans tous les villages. Nulle part on ne put songer à la résistance, nulle part on ne put trouver un lieu de refuge; les convents furent ouverts de vive force, profanés et dépouillés de tout ce qui s'y trouvait, comme on en chassait tous les habitants; même les malades dans les hôpitaux furent massacrés; les caves des maisons, les grottes dans les montagnes furent fouillées; des milliers d'hommes et de femmes furent tués dans l'intérieur de l'île et sur le rivage vis-à-vis de Psara, de sorte que la mer fut rougie au loin du sang versé et que les riches plaines étaient infectées de la peste et de l'odeur des cadavres en décomposition."—Gervinus, *Insurrection et Régénération de la Grèce*, p. 368.

PAGE 82.

The wailing of women over the dead, the μοιρολόγια, is a very old Greek custom, referred to by almost all the earlier travellers, but which is fast disappearing. Fauriel (*Chants populaires de la Grèce Moderne*, ii., p. 259) gives two examples of these mostly metrical wails, and in his very learned prefatory remarks (I. cxi.), he traces to the remotest Greek antiquity this custom, to which however he attributes a mistaken etymological explanation when writing *myriologues*.

When Priam returns from the Greek camp, bearing the corpse of Hector, the funeral rites begin with the moirologia;

Παρὰ δ' εἶσαν ἀοιδοὺς,
Θρήνων ἐξάρχους, οἵ τε στονόεσσαν ἀοιδὴν
οἱ μὲν ἄρ' ἐθρήνεον, ἐπὶ δὲ στενάχοντο γυναῖκες.
Iliad, xxiv. 720-722.

PAGE 107.

"Chios had become comparatively tranquil, only three or four murders occurring daily; the mastic villages were still respected, and carefully guarded by Elez Aga, and they had the further advantage of being exempt from a malignant fever, which, arising from the stench of so many unburied bodies, raged among the Turks. Nevertheless, troops continued to arrive from the interior of Asia, as though the isle had been an inexhaustible mine of wealth. Reinforced from Constantinople, the Capitan Pasha's fleet amounted, June the 16th, to thirty-eight sail; a fresh accession of force was promised him from the same quarter, and he expected, besides, to be joined by a powerful squadron from Alexandria, as soon as it should have accomplished its primary object of transporting an Egyptian army to Crete. The fast of Ramazan ended on Wednesday the 19th, and the Grand Admiral celebrated, on the night of the 18th, by a splendid entertainment, the approach of the moon of Bayram, which he was not fated to behold. Surrounded by the blood-stained trophies of Scio, he had forgotten the vicinity of the Greeks, who, since their previous failure, lay in the harbour of Psara, meditating a plan for his discomfiture. We have now to narrate one of the most extraordinary military exploits recorded in history, and to introduce to the reader's notice, in the person of a young Psariote sailor, the most brilliant pattern of heroism that Greece in any age has had to boast of; a heroism, too, springing from the purest motives, unalloyed by ambition or avarice. The Greeks were convinced, that if they did not by a decisive blow paralyse the Turkish fleet before its junction with that of Egypt, their islands must be exposed to imminent danger; it was proposed, therefore, in their naval council, to choose a dark night for sending in two brulots by the northern passage, while at each extremity of the strait, two ships of war should cruise in order to pick up the brulottiers. Constantine Canaris of Psara (already distinguished by his conduct at Erisso), and George Pepinos of Hydra, with thirty-two bold companions, volunteered their services; and having partaken of the holy sacrament, sailed on the 18th in two brigs, fitted up as fire-ships, and followed at the same distance by an escort of two corvettes, a brig, and a schooner. They beat to windward in the direction of Tchesmè, under French and Austrian colours, and about sunset drew so nigh to the hostile men-of-war, that they were hailed, and ordered to keep off; they tacked, accordingly, but at midnight bore off with a fresh breeze, and ran in amongst the fleet. The Psariote brulot, commanded by

Canaris, grappled the prow of the admiral's ship, anchored at the head of the line, a league from the shore, and instantly set her on fire; the Greeks then stepped into a large launch they had in tow, and passed under her poop, shouting "Victory to the Cross!" the ancient war-cry of the imperial armies of Byzantium. The Hydriotes fastened their brig to another line-of-battle ship, carrying the treasure and the Reala Bey's flag, and communicated the flames to her, but not so effectually, having applied the match a moment too soon; they were then picked up by their comrades, but the thirty-four brulottiers sailed out of the channel through the midst of the enemy without a single wound. They had, however, in their bark a barrel of gunpowder, determined to blow themselves up rather than be taken. While they departed full of joy and exultation, the roads of Scio presented an appalling sight. The Capitan Pasha's ship, which in a few minutes became one sheet of fire, contained 2286 persons, including most of the captains of the fleet, and unfortunately also a great number of Christian slaves. Not above 180 survived, for the guns going off deterred boats from approaching, and two of those belonging to the vessel foundered, from being overloaded with men endeavouring to save their lives. Although the Reala Bey's ship got clear of the Hydriote brulot, and the flames were extinguished on board of her, yet she was so seriously damaged as to be unfit for her ulterior service; and the brulot, driving about the roadstead in a state of combustion, set fire to a third two-decker, which was likewise preserved through the exertions of its crew. Overwhelmed with despair, the Capitan Pasha was placed in a launch by his attendants, but just as he seated himself there, a mast falling sank the boat, and severely bruised him; nevertheless, expert swimmers supported Kara Ala to the beach, only to draw his last breath on that spot where the Sciote hostages had suffered.

"For three quarters of an hour the conflagration blazed, casting its light far and wide over the sea and the coast of Asia, and alarming even the city of Smyrna, whose inhabitants contemplated with wonder a bright streak in the south-western sky. At two o'clock on the morning of the 19th, the flag-ship blew up with a dreadful explosion. It would be difficult to paint the consternation of the Turks; all their vessels cut their cables, some running out of the southern channel, others beating up towards the northern; if the Greek squadrons had been at hand to take advantage of their confusion, the Sultan's armament might have been annihilated. Within the isle the disorder was not less; when the admiral's ship exploded, the Mohammedans uttered lamentable cries, and most of them bent their bodies to the earth. Abdi Pasha spent the rest of the night watching by the mortal remains of the Capitan Pasha, which were interred before noon. This melancholy ceremony wound up to the highest pitch the fury of the Ottoman troops; 20,000 of them rushed into the mastic villages, killing or enslaving the people, and in spite of the resistance of Elez Aga, the 19th day of June consummated the ruin of Scio. In the month of August the total number of Christians living on that island did not exceed 1800, and the most populous village had only twelve indwellers."—*Gordon*, p. 366.

For a graphic account of Canaris's simplicity and heroic grandeur, see Count Pechio's *Une visite aux Grecs dans le Printemps de* 1825, p. 370. Canaris died September 15, 1877, while President of the Council of Ministers at Athens.

PAGE 117.

"There is not in modern annals so frightful an example of the horrors of war as that presented at Chios; it recalls us to those dark epochs when barbarous myriads rushed down on the civilised world. If it was easy for the

Porte to instil into her Asiatic subjects a thirst of vengeance, it was impossible for her to check their career, and stay the inundation. After the complete subjugation of the surviving inhabitants, not a day passed on which new bodies of Anatolian volunteers did not march into Tchesmè, whence they were wafted to the island; the sight of others who had gone before, returning with slaves and valuable spoil, stimulated their impatience, and for upwards of a month 30,000 ferocious Turks roamed about the country, hunting down miserable fugitives, and gleaning the fragments of their poverty. Elez Aga protected the mastic villages from their irruption, but four other cantons, that had equally shared the benefit of the amnesty, were ravaged by the unruly troops. A populous city, forty-six flourishing villages, and many splendid convents, reduced to ashes, attested the fierceness of Mohammedan revenge; and it was calculated at the end of May, that 25,000 Chians had fallen by the edge of the sword, and 45,000 been dragged into slavery; among the latter were the females and children of the best families. Not a few captives owed their liberation to the charity of strangers, and particularly of the [Frank] merchants of Smyrna, who, in these melancholy circumstances, forgetting their enmity to the Greeks, ransomed a multitude of prisoners; but this was, comparatively speaking, a small portion. Whole cargoes were shipped off to Constantinople, Egypt, and Barbary, and for a long period the slave-market at Smyrna displayed the bustle of active trade, and attracted Moslem purchasers from all parts of Asia Minor. The Capitan Pasha at one moment forbade the exportation of this merchandise, but as the soldiers began to put their prisoners to death, he judged it better to tolerate the abuse. About 15,000 Sciotes, mostly in a state of total destitution, escaped after the landing of the Turks; the majority of them first reached Psara, and that place not having the means to subsist them, were conveyed to other points of Greece; suffering, as they universally did, from wounds, disease, or at least hunger and nakedness, their wretched plight excited the deepest compassion. Families once opulent, and nursed in luxury, were fain to court the shelter of a ruined hovel, and to crave a morsel of bread, and many of the young women, mutilated by sabre cuts, bore testimony to the enemy's brutality. Those who fled to the consulates were saved from death or slavery; but report states that the rich were obliged to buy very dear the safeguard afforded them, and it is added that the Neapolitan consul Bogliaco, exacted from females compliances of a more humiliating description; we do not vouch for the perfect accuracy of such charges, although all Greece proclaims them, and with too much appearance of truth."—*Gordon*, p. 360.

"Même quelques consulats, et en partie ceux qui avaient sauvé le vie de tant de gens, furent accusés par l'opinion d'avoir vendu leur protection aux primats les plus riches pour de fortes sommes d'argent. Le Napolitain Boghaco fut surtout un de ces traficants d'hommes ; on le trouva plus tard, après la chute de Psara, faisant, au milieu des Turcs, le commerce du butin dans cette île où il trouva une mort violente au milieu de ces infâmes occupations. Ceux qui s'étaient sauvés dans les îles furent réduits à la pauvreté, à la mendicité et à la misère la plus affreuse. Beaucoup de Chiotes, ayant vécu dans une abondance sybaritique, avaient à peine ramassé de quoi couvrir leur nudité et de quoi prolonger leur misérable existence ; on voyait des femmes riches, vêtues de quenilles brodées d'or, dans les douleurs de l'enfantement, exposées en plein an à la chaleur du soleil et á l'humidité des nuits. Les étrangers qui virent ces lieux de désolation ne purent jamais oublier l'impression terrible que leur avaient causée l'aspect de cette île ensanglantée, ces insulaires muets d'angoisse et de douleur qui erraient encore sur la plage, de même que ceux qui, à Athénes ou à Argos, virent les Chiotes réfugiés, ne perdirent jamais le souvenir des récits déchirants que leur faisaient ces gens heureux de leur délivrance, ou hébétés par leurs malheurs ou respirant la vengeance. Une nombreuse population avait été frappée d'un châtiment tel que, dans les temps modernes, les éléments aveugles en ont seuls infligé aux hommes ; il fut prouvé ainsi, par un exemple tout récent, que, dans les masses du peuple turc, la barbarie la plus ancienne d'une nature à demi bestiale n'était pas encore éteinte. Quand l'histoire nous offre des spectacles aussi effrayants et aussi émouvants, on ne peut chercher une consolation que dans leurs résultats et dans leur signification au milieu de l'enchainement général des événements. Le désastre horrible, cette fureur infâme dechainée contre une population fidèle, douce, inoffensive et innocente, et cette violation insolente d'une promesse de grâce et de modération publiquement proclamée et garantie, servirent, plus que toute autre chose, à aider l'opinion publique, en Europe, à se prononcer definitivement sur cette lutte terrible de deux peuples en apparence également barbares, et où les cruautés commises des deux côtés avaient pendant longtemps tenu les âmes consciencieuses dans l'incertitude et dans le doute. On reconnut qu'on n'avait pas seulement affaire à des ennemies de la chrêtienté, mais aux ennemis de toute nature humaine et de toute humanité."—*Gervinus*, p. 371.

Delacroix' famous picture *Le Massacre de*

Chio, now in the Louvre, has popularised in France this tragic episode of the Greek war of Liberation.

PAGE 120.

" We have seen that in 1821 the Motesellim had taken hostages, whose number was augmented by degrees to fourscore. Vehib Pasha subsequently despatched four of them to Constantinople, but when the Samians disembarked he still kept in custody seventy-six of the principal citizens, including the archbishop and the heads of the clergy. These men were clearly innocent. So far from stimulating rebellion, they had done all in their power to prevent it, and had by their letters contributed to the pacification of the Masticokhoria, and to Logotheti's expulsion. Yet, as soon as they had performed that service they were executed with every mark of ignominy, and their remains thrown into the waves, where, with shoals of other dead bodies, they floated around the Ottoman vessels. There is reason to believe that a direct order from the Sultan prescribed this atrocity, because at the same time the four hostages at Constantinople, and seven or eight Sciote merchants settled in the capital were put to death. The flimsy allegation brought forward to justify the perpetration of so shocking a piece of barbarity, was that two primates sent into the country by Vehib Pasha, when he learned Lycurgus' approach to calm the minds of the peasants, had joined the insurgents, as they could not help doing, their retreat to the castle being cut off by the precipitate flight of the Turkish detachments."— *Gordon*, p. 362.

PAGE 126.

Nicolas Mavroyenis was dragoman of the fleet under Admiral Hassan-Pasha, who subdued the Morea after the revolt provoked by the Russians in 1770. He was appointed Hospodar of Walachia in 1786. In March 1789 he was decapitated by the Turks on the pretext that he had contributed to their defeat by the Austrians at the battle of Kalafat. (See *Memoir du Mavroyenis* by G. Antonopoulos in the Βέρων of 1878, p. 305.) The name of the young and beautiful Miss Mavroyenis is mentioned in the works of most of the Philhellenes who visited Greece during the Revolution. (See Rayband, *Memoires sur les Grèce*, Paris, 1825; and *Mavrogénie, ou l'héroine de la Grèce, nouvelle historique et contemporaine, suivie d'une lettre de l'héroine aux dames Parisiennes*, par T. Ginouvier, Paris, 1825.)

Page 127.

"L'île de Tinos est aujourd'hui (1824) la plus agréable et la plus florissante des Cyclades . . . . . ce fut la dernière possession des Vénitiens dans l'Archipel ; ils ne l'évacuèrent qu'en 1714. . . . Les Tiniotes se croyaient à l'abri de tout danger, parce qu'ils étaient délivrés de leur Aga et de ses trois jannissaires . . . . San Nicolo (la capitale de l'île) a vu sa population s'augmenter, depuis la guerre, d'un grand nombre de familles qui s'y sont réfugiées . . . . Les Tiniotes sont extrêmement portés au plaisir. Les femmes y jouissent d'une plus grande liberté que dans aucune autre partie de la Gréce. . . . Leur passion pour la danse est extrême ; nous approchions du carnaval ; elles consacraient à cet amusement de nuits entières et une partie des jours. On dansait à Tinos, on égorgeait ailleurs." *Rayband*, ii. p. 124. See also "L'île de Tinos," by Alexis de Vallon in the *Revue des Deux Mondes*, June 1st, 1843. This article has been translated into Greek and published at Tinos ; for the island is now possessed of a printing press and a journal.

Page 141.

The Mills, Οἱ Μύλοι, is the name of a small haven facing the town of Nauplia ; it was the port used by the Greek army investing the fortress.

Page 142.

"Quelque temps seulement avant l'insurrection, Négris avait été nommé chargé d'affaires de la Porte à Paris; apprenant, en ce rendant à Marseille, l'explosion de la révolte, fidèle à ses compatriotes, mais infidèle à son maître, il avait jeté ses lettres de créance à la mer pour embrasser la cause de la révolte. Petit, maigre, timide de sa nature, mais rendu hardi par l'ambition, il était un des hommes les plus habiles, les plus rusés, les plus actifs, mais aussi des plus versatiles de l'école diplomatique des Grecs."—*Gervinus*, p. 324.

Negris was born at Constantinople, towards the end of the last century. He first served as Secretary-General under Callimachis, Hospodar of Walachia. He died from typhus at Nauplia, on the 22d of March 1824. Finlay (i. p. 356) thus relates the adventures of his library:—

"The small but choice library of Theodore Negris, the Secretary of State, was carried off on a stolen horse by a Maniat soldier. The horse fell lame; the Maniat then sold it for two dollars to an officer, who bought it to carry water to his soldiers, who were posted on the hill above Lerna; to his surprise he found himself in possession of a library. Some days after, the books came into the possession of Captain Hastings, who informed Negris of the fate of his library; but that restless politician never expressed a wish to repossess them, perhaps never afterwards had a place where he thought them safe."

Page 144.

The convention for the surrender of the Nauplia was signed on June 18, 1822. But the besieged protracted the negotiations in the hope that Dram-Ali's expedition would not only save the fortress, but completely subjugate Greece. His army, thirty thousand strong, crossed the Sperchios on the 29th of that month, and was advancing southward, when, on the 26th of July, the Greeks, under Colocotronis, annihilated the Turkish host in the defile of Derwen, near Corinth. That famous victory saved Greece. The siege of Nauplia was recommenced. The town resisted until the morning of 12th December, the festival of St. Andreas, when Staïkos, with a handful of devoted men, captured the citadel of Palamidi.

Page 145.

"—12 Août 1829. Nauplie est une petite ville assez bien bâtie, située entre le pied du mont Palamède et la mer. Les rues sont droites et dallées, les maisons assez belles. Les grands magasins bâtis par les Vénitiens existent encore. La ville est devenue le siège du gouvernement. Capodistria commence à y faire construire un bel hôtel pour les affaires d'Etat. Les femmes adoptent déja les modes parisiennes, et les hommes le frac et le pantalon. Quel sacrilège!"—*Notes sur la Grèce*, par Lucien Davesiès de Pontès, Paris, 1864, p. 162.

Page 149.

"On the 20th September, the Ottoman fleet, consisting of eighty sail, including transports, was descried from the beacon of Hydra, and on the following morning the Capitan-Pasha stood on towards the island of Spetzæ with a fair wind, and the gulf of Nauplia open before him. The Greek fleet, consisting of sixty sail, chiefly brigs of from eight to fourteen guns, stood out to engage the Turks."—Finlay, i. p. 165.

Page 173.

"From Syra the Capitan Pasha steered towards Mycone, which the natives mostly quitted, seeking a refuge at Tinos; 400 men who remained, seemed to court an attack by their bravadoes and insults to the Islamite faith. A detachment of 100 Algerines landed for the purpose of taking cattle, but, being vigorously assailed by the Myconiotes, were driven off, leaving seventeen dead behind them, while the Greeks had but two wounded: the Ottoman admiral did not think proper to avenge this affront. At Tinos the view of the hostile fleet excited the utmost enthusiasm, not less than 7000 men preparing to defend themselves to the last extremity; their courage, however, was not put to the test, for the Turks proceeded to Tenedos, and anchored there to await the Sultan's orders."—*Gordon*, 1, p. 468.

PAGE 185.

In most of the Greek islands the sound of κ before the vowels ε, ι, υ, and the diphthongs of the same value, becomes as soft almost as the italian *c* before *e* and *i*. In like manner γ and χ are pronounced as gutturals before ο and α, whereas they become soft before the above-mentioned vowels.

PAGE 186.

The local magistrates in Chio and in most of the other parts of Greece were called δημογέροντες, elders of the commune. This is a very ancient designation, being employed in the same sense in Homer: *Iliad*, III. 149, xi. 372. Also Euripides' *Andromaché*, v. 300.

PAGE 197.

"Masticochoria" is the name given collectively to the 22 villages situated in the southern part of the island, where the mastic is produced, as stated in the Note to p. 4.

Printed by R. & R. CLARK, *Edinburgh.*

www.ingramcontent.com/pod-product-compliance
Lightning Source LLC
Chambersburg PA
CBHW032055220426
43664CB00008B/1011